TAKE THIS ADVICE

TAKE THIS ADVICE

THE MOST NAKEDLY HONEST GRADUATION SPEECHES EVER GIVEN

EDITED BY SANDRA BARK

SIMON SPOTLIGHT ENTERTAINMENT

New York London Toronto Sydney

SIMON SPOTLIGHT ENTERTAINMENT
An imprint of Simon & Schuster
1230 Avenue of the Americas, New York, New York 10020
Manufactured in the United States of America
First Edition 10 9 8 7 6 5 4 3 2 1
Library of Congress Cataloging-in-Publication Data
Take this advice : the most nakedly honest graduation speeches ever given / edited by
Sandra Bark.—1st ed.
p. cm.
ISBN 0-689-87849-4 (alk. paper)
1. Baccalaureate addresses. 2. Speeches, addresses, etc., American. 3. Speeches,
addresses, etc., English. 4. College graduates—Conduct of life. I. Bark, Sandra.
PS663.C74T35 2005
815'.008—dc22
2004026233

Copyright information is continued on pages 224 and 225.

TAKE THIS ADVICE

CONTENTS

PUBLIC FIGURES

WRITERS

ACTORS

An actress can only play a woman.
I'm an actor, I can play anything.

—*Whoopi Goldberg*

ROBERT REDFORD

Bard College, 2004

Though I hold a somewhat nontraditional background of academic scholarship and credentials, I wondered, in preparation of coming here today, what gemlike bits of knowledge I could offer . . . when it seems as if only yesterday I was being asked to leave college! Despite a rather unfortunate history of schooling, I nonetheless developed an acute interest in education and its value in inspiring an active critical mindset.

I imagine many will want to give you advice as you embark on the next phase of your lives. While I'd like to say I'm not one of them, I'll be no different. What I can do is share with you personal observations and thoughts from a good portion of the life I've experienced—the life I've lived—and reflect on what I think lies ahead, what power and control over it I believe you have, and in essence, what I wish for you.

I have children. Grandchildren. Grew up during the Second World War when we believed it was a just and humanitarian cause. And we were right, we were united. I knew what it felt like to, as a country, pull together in a time of crisis, as class and race distinctions fell by the wayside in a solid show of that unity. Though my family shared with countless others the loss of members, the love of country—*our* country—as well as the principles it was founded upon remain steadfast. It's more

3

complicated nowadays, and while I don't want to dwell on the turmoil of the world today, it can't be like the big elephant sitting in the room that we don't acknowledge.

The world you are entering upon completion of your scholarship, although more advanced and developed, is also more complicated and smaller. In all of these tenuous times there's been a pattern about the political gains of not telling the truth, and the pattern is not always a good one. America has long had the distinction of going to the brink and pulling itself out at the last moment. Some from my lifetime: two world wars, starting with the Great Depression; the civil rights movement; Cuban missile crisis; Vietnam; there was McCarthyism; the Iran-Contra scandal; and Watergate and Nixon, to name a handful. It feels like we're again on the edge, and if there has ever been a time when voices need to be raised in unison around the kind of America and the kind of world we want for you and your children, it's now.

The world I was born into held some very sacred notions. There were laws and rights that protected and advanced us, such as the Freedom of Information Act, the Environmental Policy Act, or the controversial Roe versus Wade. My generation has set examples, both good and bad. It's funny that our country is brimming with positive impulse but awash in contradiction. We put a man on the moon for the first time, yet we'll be the first generation to leave the natural world, the environment, in worse shape than when we got here. We enacted historic civil and human rights laws and environmental protections, yet today, just about all of them are again in play politically. We created a free and thriving press, with standards and practices that ensured balance and fairness, though we now grapple with the blur and bias of news as entertainment and entertainment as news. We built a great and proud and economically thriving America, but we must constantly revisit repercussions of "progress," and the price future generations, including yours, must pay for it. While some of the greatest medical and technological advancements of mankind have been developed by my generation, still a huge portion of the world's people live in dire straights, and world peace has never been more elusive.

One of the things that will always be inevitable is change, full of both vague uncertainty and brilliant promise. I don't have to tell you, as you are a technological generation, that modes of communication and information flow that we currently use will be passé by tomorrow. That's a given. What's not a given is how humanity will fare in all of this. Global society as a whole will only be more balanced and more equitable depending upon your success in playing an active role, along with being mindful of the human consequence of it all. Though our nation's security is as important as international relations, a broader sense of defense is being ignored. Of course you can't compete on a world stage through a veil of wishful thinking, but you can defend against threats to our natural resources, civil liberties, and the like. Turning your knowledge and skills toward these things will nurture peace in your lives and in the world. This can certainly be as noble and right as simply inventing or searching for the next great weapon of mass destruction. Diplomacy, engagement, understanding other cultures, and exercising some humility along with your strength is another form of defense.

To build a sustainable society on every level is the only true answer, and we all have a role to play in it. You are most important because you are just beginning your life journey. It's all interconnected in an ongoing rhythm—creativity, environment, culture, politics, economics, and the lot—and it is success or failure at this which will determine what your lives will be like in the future. Keeping creativity alive, and learning from past experience, while nurturing new ideas, new ways of looking at old challenges, thinking outside the box—are critical to the success of truly sustainable solutions and ways of life. Let's face it, creativity is at the core of everything . . . from the latest medical discovery to the next technological advancement—not just beloved symphonies, films, or paintings. Creativity is at the core of rhythm. Furthering that rhythm is the chance to make sure all facets of a sustainable future are employed, for many . . . not few.

I'm not a big fan of centralization. I believe individuality and diversity are the backbone and strength of our country, and its benefits shouldn't be squandered. I started the Sundance Institute because I felt new ideas, new voices—those not readily accepted or just beginning to form—needed a place to breathe and grow. I felt that raw, authentic visions might benefit from an environment where taking risks was embraced, and where the freedom to fail could be seen as a step in growth and development. But most importantly I wanted the experience to be a place where free expression always had a home and creativity thrived. And if we were lucky, we'd succeed in finding ways to get those voices out to as wide an audience as possible. There has been some success in that regard, unlike the first few years of the Sundance Film Festival when I was standing out on street corners with other festival staff members trying to get people just to go into the theaters to watch the films. A few folks even tried to haggle: "I will if you sit in there with me!"

I discovered and used art in my life because in addition to my soul's vocation, it represented the most accessible path to independent spirit and thinking. Yet still, on this very day, freedom of expression is threatened in more ways than it should be . . . under siege if you will. Since when is a film, a play, a photograph, a painting so threatening that it should be locked away in the dark, never to see the light of day? We can go to war based in part on lies, but not have in the public domain art that debated its strengths or weaknesses? It's wrong and it's dangerous, and your generation must not only take note, but also take action to stop this slide. It's your right. It's your future.

In the almost thirty years since Watergate, many of our systems of checks and balances have been infected by everything from media consolidation and greed to limited ideologies and *apathy*. As well, there's an underlying lack of balance when those in power don't invite debate, saying instead that we are somehow lesser Americans to question their actions. There's something wrong when we're forced to go to court for the release of information that rightly should be public in a free democracy. Why should we have to fight so hard for truths that are our right to have? Knowledge is the foundation on which *advancing* societies are based, and our country possesses a beauty and scope unmatched: exciting, still broad, full of strength and fragility.

One of the reasons this country is so great and has lasted so long is that the laws of the land set in motion some two hundred years ago were meant to nurture stability, diversity, and fairness to all, and to a large degree this has worked. But dissent must be as passionately protected as conformity, and I would hope your generation embraces this fervently.

The founding doctrine of our country, the Constitution, can and does come under threat, and that's one thing we cannot let happen. Some of these systems have witnessed an effort to erase them. They'll have to be put back together, and *you can* put them back. You can participate by being a force in the power of collective action and raising a voice so loud that it can't be denied. We need to regain our purpose and dignity as a nation, and that can also be accomplished through individual action. Don't turn off if you become fed up. *Value* freedom of speech and expression. It will be your charge to ensure they stay safe for your kids and theirs. As much as anyone's, your future is shaped by current events.

While we live with the consequences of policies that affect our well-being—the air we breathe, what water we drink, the schools our kids attend and the education they deserve, our role on the world stage—we can still be called unpatriotic when we disagree with those policies. Why is that? Making choices based solely on political "strategy" rather than attempting to create a harmony of sorts sets a dangerous precedent for democracy. Sustained by narrow ideology and a propensity toward squelching healthy debate and dialogue, we must overcome the current you're-either-with-us-or-against-us philosophy of those with the traditional modes of power. And we can. As new graduates, you are engaged in seeking a bright future and will see past the transparencies of such dangerous behavior.

Someone once asked me what was the best thing to do to become an actor. I said, "Pay attention." The same goes for you in your chosen professional fields. You have an opportunity to have a voice, but you have to feel it, want it in everyday life. Then you have to fight for it. Demand it. Be courageous in the expression of your beliefs, whatever they might be. Scandals in high places have surely disillusioned and disenfranchised, but don't roll over. Don't be sheep—be lions. Don't lose sight of the big picture just because savvy communicators know how to divert your attention from it. It's true that with so many means of communication coming at you at any given time, you have to work harder to focus on the big picture. But look *above* the details, look past the miasma of partisan hype—the trees, if you will—and see the woods. Step back.

It's easy to be led by slogans and sound bites on the nightly news. In fact, we are besieged by them. But it's in your interest to look beyond the spin. Spin—tear the heart out of the Clean Air Act? Call it the Healthy Skies Initiative. Destroy national forests owned by the citizens of this country? Call it the Healthy Forest Initiative. Turn a deaf ear to families dealing with pollution-induced asthma in favor of corporate polluters? Why not? A little more arsenic in the water isn't such a big deal as we "leave no child behind." Look carefully and deeply. You will see patterns that have roots in similar mindsets of the past, e.g., Nixon and Watergate. The hands of time cannot be turned back. We must adjust to the era we are living in with a time of new ideas, new minds . . . you.

For example, I know we all value having the right to vote, but I think it's important to reflect on the fact that it didn't come easily. Voting is an opportunity that comes with living in a free society, a democracy. I read recently that in South Africa some 93 percent of young people of voting age participated in their first free election, and in America 16 percent of young people voted in the 2000 elections. More people voted on American Idol than they did in the midterm election. In the clang and clutter of the current media hype, it's not easy. It takes a bit of time to try to become informed on where a candidate stands and what the dynamics of particular issues on the ballot might be. But the world over, people have fought, suffered, even died in their quest for this right, and maybe we take that right to vote for granted. Maybe we've become a bit spoiled.

I'm an optimist, a dark one to be sure, with great pulses of cynicism, but an optimist. It keeps me going. I believe in the potential good. Cynicism is easy, a cheat, a dead end. Skepticism is healthy, but cynicism, no. It's a cop-out. You're a cynic and what is left behind? Nothing. An optimist—even a somewhat skeptical optimist—someone who's engaged, can look back and perhaps see something left behind as a result of his or her efforts.

So here we are, a time "between a no longer and a not yet," amidst years of danger and promise, and we can only hope, as educator and political philosopher Hannah Arendt did, that the "tug toward apathy will be overcome by the lure of human improvement and preservation." We need public engagement and collective action more now than ever. We have become a divided country. It shouldn't be. Ask yourselves why. Look hard. Why should we be at war with art, the environment, and education? Is this America as we envisioned it? As we hope and believe it should be? No.

If I can leave you with one thought today at this critical juncture in your lives and that of the world, it would be to hold to your true selves. Realize the tremendous opportunities available to you and trust in yourselves as you use individual ingenuity to define your life and role in the world. Don't be hindered in times that can be full of angst, confusion, and chaos; it is also an exciting period considering what this country can instill and present to you as you shape and play your role in the future. It is a wonderful, beautiful country, still capable of reaching its potential, to itself and the world, ever capable of expressing the virtues of democracy and freedom.

It's moving into your hands, and that is truly exciting. It is a gift in a way. How many other countries are equipped to give their young a platform so full of richness? It's your world to inherit and move forward. I have learned in my experience, the climb up . . . *that* is where there is much to be found. I know you can and will. I have faith in you. I have no choice.

As Robert Frost once wrote:

> *"Two Tramps in Mud Time" (1936)*
> *But yield who will to their separation,*
> *My object in living is to unite*
> *My avocation and my vocation*
> *As my two eyes make one in sight.*
> *Only where love and need are one,*
> *And the work is play for mortal stakes,*
> *Is the deed ever really done*
> *For Heaven and the future's sakes.*

That is my wish for you.

Robert Redford has received international acclaim as an actor, director, and producer, as well as for his work as a champion of independent film.

CHRISTOPHER REEVE

Middlebury College, 2004

President McCardell, trustees, faculty, students and staff, ladies and gentlemen. I'm extremely honored to become a Doctor of Humane Letters. If I could just torture the meaning of the phrase for a second, actually most of the letters I write are not very humane. Usually they're sharply critical of somebody, or I'm asking for money.

Many of you graduating today are probably apprehensive about your entry into the real world. That's completely understandable. Sometimes I harbor a secret desire to be kidnapped by aliens and taken to a planet more sensible than this one. But time and again hope is renewed by the actions of ordinary people.

A couple of examples come to mind. The formation of the 9-11 Commission was largely due to the courage and persistence of the families and friends of the victims. In a television interview, one family member said that in 2001 all she knew about the federal government was that there was a House and a Senate, but she wasn't sure what they did. (I think many Americans would like an answer to that one too.) She literally didn't know how our government works. And yet she and others like her got together, educated themselves, and had a significant impact on the investigation of one of the most critical moments in American history.

In the early eighties the public discourse about AIDS was

divisive and ugly. Some elected officials said the disease was God's revenge on people who lived a certain lifestyle. The federal government wouldn't fund the search for a cure. Today the NIH spends $1.8 billion on AIDS research annually, and the virus is no longer an epidemic in this country.

How did we move from that climate of fear and animosity in the early eighties to where we are today? It was by the extraordinary efforts of ordinary individuals who created a grassroots movement. Then change occurred, as it has time and time again throughout our history.

All of you who are leaving Middlebury today are uniquely qualified to effect change and movement in our society. Never underestimate the difference you can make. I've learned by being literally paralyzed that to a large extent, paralysis is a choice. We can either watch life from the sidelines, or actively participate. We can rationalize inaction by deciding that one voice or one vote doesn't matter, or we can make the choice that inaction is unacceptable. Either we let self-doubt and feelings of inadequacy prevent us from realizing our potential, or we embrace the fact that when we turn our attention away from ourselves, our potential is limitless.

Some people have to be pushed to the edge or confront their own mortality in order to gain that perspective, to learn to live a more conscious and fearless life. But you don't have to do that. You don't have to go to the edge, and you can choose not to be paralyzed. Whether or not you realize it right now, the education you have received here has prepared you to pursue your own ambitions without losing sight of the invaluable difference you can make in this world.

As you go forward I hope you won't forget that. It may be difficult, because you will encounter corruption and chaos. You will have to bring your personal integrity with you on the journey because you may not find anyone to guide you. But don't be afraid, and never give up. Just listen to the voice inside you—the voice of honesty we all have within us—that will tell you, if you let it, that you're heading in the right direction.

Congratulations on all you've achieved so far. I wish you the best of luck. Thank you very much.

Actor, director, and activist Christopher Reeve passed away in October 2004 at the age of fifty-two, just months after delivering this speech. Paralyzed in an equestrian accident in 1995, he spent the rest of his life working to encourage the medical community to pay closer attention to spinal cord injuries.

MERYL STREEP

University of New Hampshire, 2003

ood morning, Governor Benson, President Hart, members of the Board of Trustees, distinguished faculty, proud parents, and you, almost alumni. I'm very pleased to be here today to address you on this day, your last day of wearing your tassels on the left. I have agonized over this speech, mostly because I don't usually give speeches, or when I do, it's at my house, and nobody listens. I have thought long and hard about how to advise you, inspire you, thrill and excite you over multiple speakers that repeat each word-erd-erd in that sonic-onic-onic Doppler-oppler-oppler effect-ect-ect that makes you want to go to sleep-eep-eep. Meryl Streep-eep-eep put me to sleep-eep-eep. Probably quite a few of you need a great deal of sleep after all of the parties, er, studying, finals, and things of Senior Spring. And if you're at all like my college-age children, you're used to getting most of your sleep during daylight hours . . . am I right?

Because I want you not to doze, I decided I should avoid politics. Also, of course, I am in show business, and not allowed to speak about politics. Or, I'm allowed to speak, of course I'm allowed to speak, and never work again. But my problem is: I've never heard of anybody making anything but a political speech in New Hampshire. Nobody makes a speech in New Hampshire unless they're stumping for something, do they? I think it's a state law, isn't it? Your honor? If I have to, by law, make a political speech, you'll sleep. But if I make a speech about sex, you'll wake up. See, it's already working! So I'll make a speech about sexual politics, and I won't be running for anything except, perhaps, cover.

I went to school in New Hampshire thirty years ago as one of the first women to integrate Dartmouth College. We were sixty intrepid girls on a campus of approximately six thousand men. We tried to lead them, gently, toward a difficult idea (one that UNH has endorsed almost since its inception): the idea that women are valuable to a university. It was not as difficult as convincing the Taliban more recently of the same thing, but I do remember some pitched battles back then. Your graduation class today of nearly three thousand students is almost 2-to-1 women, and your school is not an anomaly. This imbalance, to differing degrees, is replicated at colleges and universities around the country. In the huge University of California system, women are in a strong majority, averaging around 57 percent of the student population. According to Peterson's Guide, at NYU and Boston University, the percentage is 60-40 women to men. What's going on? And who, thirty years ago, would've ever predicted it? (Maybe the Taliban had a legitimate fear: Give them an inch and they'll just take over!)

These statistics are all the more confusing when we acknowledge the fact that the glass ceiling is still in effect in the business world, the professions, and politics. Imagine if the Senate were apportioned in the same way as your graduating class! Or that there were twice as many women as men in the House!? Or the White House! Or on cable news!? At the heads of Fortune 500 companies? It's almost unimaginable. You can scan the mastheads of major news organizations, the lists of the top echelons of business and management, the hierarchies of power in government, and it still reads pretty much like it did in the middle of the last century, or the century before that, or the centuries before that. In other words, it's like the membership list of the Augusta Golf Club today.

Why is there this discrepancy between how many women succeed in college and where they actually end up? What happens to all these people after graduation? Back in 1970 we thought that if we had access to the same educational opportunities as men, then the same opportunities would naturally present themselves out in the Real World. We've more than crashed through the first, the educational barrier, but the other is proving tougher to go up against. It may seem as if universities are optimistically and successfully preparing an unprecedented number of female students for leadership opportunities that don't exist. Many women will confront the attitude of top PGA golfer Vijay Singh when he declared he would rather quit the tournament than play alongside the top-ranked woman in the country. At the highest levels of achievement some men still find humiliation in competing (and potentially coming up short) against women. Why does it hurt more to lose to a girl, unless, deep down, you think girls are worth less than boys? This is an old and deep-seated and in many cases unconscious prejudice; you can circle the globe and find its gnarly roots wrapped around the foundations of many societies. And just like any other prejudice, cultural or racial, it'll take a long time for it to die out. But shrivel it will, because it's basically a negative, regressive, underground impulse that cannot live in the light of a new day. As we continue to see, societies that look backward and keep their women down fail to keep pace in the modern world. We know from our own eighty-year battle to claim our rights that the

Founding Fathers weren't thinking of women when they wrote the concept of freedom into our Constitution. But you could argue that part of the reason that the West has sustained its ascendancy is due to the exponentially expanding opportunities offered ALL of its citizens.

You, the gentlemen of the graduating class, have experienced life on campus as members of the minority. I hope they didn't give you too hard a time. At least this may have given you an appreciation for the importance of preserving the rights of the few; democracy is devoted to the idea that everyone, not just the majority, deserves a voice. My brothers were taught as boys to open the door for the ladies, a practice they were happy to forget about in the advent of the women's movement. At the leadership level now, however, chivalry of a new sort is called for. I hope when you encounter the success you deserve, and the discrepancy I have talked about, you will respond with speed and grace. The door should be opened for the ladies, the boardroom door, and our gentlemen will have to do it.

We all need to be given opportunities, and then we have to disregard all of the statistics that predict we're not likely to reach our goal. Success is often provided by the exception to the Rules for Success. People who have broken through color and gender lines, class and cultural bias, have done so despite an array of reasons as to why they shouldn't be able to do so. In this way, success may ultimately have more to do with your own personality, focus, and optimism than your gender, race, or background. Put blinders on to those things that conspire to hold you back, especially the ones in your own head. Guard your good mood. Listen to music every day, joke, and love and read more for fun, especially poetry.

And now I'm going to read you a poem, because I believe that every solemn, joyous, tedious, and important rite of passage should and must be celebrated and elevated by poetry. This is "Begin," by Brendan Kennelly.

> *Begin again to the summoning birds*
> *to the sight of light at the window,*
> *begin to the roar of morning traffic*
> *all along Pembroke Road.*
> *Every beginning is a promise*
> *born in light and dying in dark determination*
> *and exaltation of springtime*
> *flowering the way to work.*
> *Begin to the pageant of queuing girls*
> *the arrogant loneliness of swans in the canal*
> *bridges linking the past and the future*
> *old friends passing through with us still.*
> *Begin to the loneliness that cannot end*
> *since it perhaps is what makes us begin,*
> *begin to wonder at unknown faces*
> *at crying birds in the sudden rain*
> *at branches stark in the willing sunlight*
> *at seagulls foraging for bread*
> *at couples sharing a sunny secret*
> *alone together while making good.*
> *Though we live in a world that dreams of ending*
> *that always seems about to give in*
> *something that will not acknowledge conclusion*
> *insists that we forever begin.*

And lastly, as to the whole sad thing with the Old Man of the Mountain; two hundred years ago, Daniel Webster remarked of the rocky crag: "God has hung out a sign to show that in New England he makes Men." I say, "Hmmm . . . maybe God is changing the sign." Mountains can crumble, but our love will remain.

I speak for all here who send you out into your future with love, respect for your hard work, and high happy hopes for each and every one of you. Good luck, and thank you.

Meryl Streep is a recipient of two Oscars, five Golden Globes, and an Emmy for her outstanding work on the screen and on television.

COMEDIANS

*Perhaps the mission of those who love
mankind is to make people laugh at the truth.*

—Umberto Eco

BILL COSBY

The Juilliard School, 2002

S ome of you will understand and feel the story I'm about to tell; others will just enjoy the story. First of all, I'm very proud to be accepted into this wonderful family along with my uncle, Samuel Russell Cosby Jr. [BS '48, MS '50].

When I decided to become a stand-up comedian, I was very sure of myself. I wrote the monologues and I performed them. I felt that they were different, and people told me that the monologues were, in fact, different—because they said that they weren't funny! I would perform the monologue to show the person where the "funny" was, and the person would say, "It's still not funny," so I decided to do it myself. And having played football for Temple University, I had no fear of losing.

I was working for sixty dollars a week, seven days a week, at a place called the Gaslight Café at 116 MacDougal Street. They served espresso. (I'm from North Philadelphia, a lower income area; we knew nothing about espresso or paying two dollars for a cup of coffee, but people are crazy when they're in college.) I went to work from 8 P.M. to 4 A.M., and my job description was to break up the monotony of the folk singers. My time onstage varied from five minutes to two hours. I dropped out of school my junior year, disappointing my mother and father, but I just could not continue to sit in the classroom and drift; it just didn't do anything for me. I had to get out and see.

Two gentlemen came to the Gaslight Café: twin brothers named Marienthal, George and Oscar. They were from Chicago. There was another fellow, Alan Ribback, who owned the Gate of Horn in Chicago. Alan Ribback looked at the Marienthal brothers and said, "I want this guy." And something happened to me then that had never happened in my life before: I was going to fly to Chicago. The guy sent me a round-trip ticket and paid me one hundred fifty dollars a week (I was making sixty dollars a week at the Gaslight Café). I thought, "This is show biz! I'm already ahead of the game. I've made more money than my father made last year!" So I go out to the Gate of Horn (a folk room which seated 135 people), and I open for Oscar Brown Jr. Oscar and I sold the place out. The announcer says, "And now, one of the leading Negro comedians in the world, Mr. Bill Cosby!"

I come out, I've got thirty-five minutes of material planned; I don't get into any of it. I ad-lib and the people fall out of their chairs. They're loving me; I'm loving them. And I do two weeks there. Alan Ribback brings me back in August and I open for a group called the Terriers. I do the same thing; I just have a ball.

Then an offer came from Mister Kelly's, right across the street, and this is the room. Now, every big-name comic played that room: Jackie Leonard, Shelly Berman, Mort Sahl, Lenny Bruce, George Kirby, Dick Gregory, and others. These guys are making twenty-five hundred dollars a week. The guy offered me seven hundred fifty dollars to play this room in October, plus the ticket to get there. I accept.

I check into the Maryland Hotel and I go to Mister Kelly's. Now, you've got to keep in mind that, in my mind, this is IT. I've heard about this place; it's an icon, it has tremendous aura. The Marienthal brothers greet me, they ask me if I wanted to rehearse, and I say, "There is no need to rehearse." There were two shows, at 8 P.M. and midnight.

I go up to my dressing room and I start to talk to myself about whether I should really be in this room. "Am I funny enough to be here?" And I answered myself: "Yes, I am." Then I said to myself, "You know these guys are tremendous, and this audience knows the greats." And I said, "Yes, I know that." Then I said, "Yeah, but across the street is a different thing; those are college kids, they'll laugh at anything. These are grown people, these are drinking people! Some of them are not happy with their lives. Face it, these people want more than college people—these people have responsibilities. And I don't think you're funny enough for these people. I don't know why you accepted this job; you've got a lot of nerve coming in here."

For four hours, I ran myself into a mental situation where I really knew I was not funny. I knew I had no business being in this room. And so the time came, and Mr. Marienthal came up and said, "Good luck." And I said, "Thank you." And then I said to myself, "Forget about it."

The place, which seats about 240 people, was packed, and the trio was playing. The announcer said, "Ladies and gentlemen, Mister Kelly's is proud to present one of the leading new faces on the comedy horizon, Mr. Bill Cosby Jr." And I go out and look at this crowd, and my first thought is: "I'm not funny. These people are not going to laugh." I proceeded to do a thirty-five-minute act in eighteen minutes. I don't remember if I had "flop sweat." I just remember that when I said, "Thank you and good night," they all said, "Yes!"

I walked off and went upstairs and sat in my dressing room. I was not sick in the stomach; I just felt that I made a terrible mistake. This was not what I wanted to do, and I didn't know how I talked myself into this. I want to go back to Temple University and apologize to Professor Sapolsky; I'm going to get my master's and my doctorate and all this foolishness is over. And the Marienthal brothers came in, and George said to Oscar, "Wait outside." I'm sitting there looking at the trash basket, and I said, "Mr. Marienthal, just let me tell you this right now: I am going home. You don't have to pay me; I will use the ticket to get home. I will pay the hotel bill, and I'm just sorry about everything and the way it worked out. That's it, sir." And he looked at me and said, "Good. You go back to the hotel and you pack and you go home. And send Bill Cosby back here. I don't know why he sent you, because you stink. I hired Bill Cosby, and I don't know who you are, but you get out. Go tell Bill Cosby if he's not back here by the twelve o'clock show, I'm suing him and I'm going to have someone beat him up. But you, son—you need to go back to college and get your degree. I imagine you're a nice person, but you're not a comedian. You stink! And I don't know why he gave you his material; you messed it up, you were absolutely horrible." And he walked out.

After hearing that, I didn't feel any better. I can't tell you why I just sat there until the twelve o'clock show. I was just as depressed and I was really trying to fight it. I kept saying, "I can't do it. I'm not good."

I stood in the dark waiting to go onstage. The announcer said, "And now, ladies and gentlemen, Bill Cosby." And I said, "What happened to 'the leading new comedian'?" And he said, "Did you see the last show?" I started talking—talking back to him, and the audience started laughing, and that was just the beginning. We went back and forth and I did thirty-five minutes like I was at the Gaslight Café in Greenwich Village.

This might sound like a joke, but it isn't: Had Juilliard taught me, I think I would have given a different performance at Mister Kelly's. Because I would have been sure of myself and that's who you are.

My message to those of you who may doubt yourselves is the following: The day that you go for an audition and you decide not to show up, that's the job you lose. When you go to an audition, you show up and you do it, and it's always going to be a wonderful experience. There's no excuse worse than, "Well, I went, but I was so nervous I blew it." Why go? It is my pleasure to stand here and tell you that, each and every time you go for it, make sure you take yourself—because that's who they asked to see.

Thank you.

In his forty-year career Bill Cosby, America's most beloved humorist, has gone from nightclub comic to television star to international personality.

WILL FERRELL

Harvard University, Class Day, 2003

This is not the Worcester, Mass., Boat Show, is it? I am sorry. I have made a terrible mistake. Ever since I left *Saturday Night Live,* I mostly do public speaking now. And I must have made an error in the little Palm Pilot. Boy. Don't worry. I got it on me. I got the speech on me. Let's see. Ah, yes. Here we go.

You know, when Bill Gates first called me to speak to you today, I was honored. But when he wanted me to be one of the Roxbury guys, I—Sorry, that's Microsoft. I'm sorry about that. Star Trek Convention. No. NRA. NAACP. Dow Chemical. No. But that is a good one. That is a good speech. The University of Michigan Law. Johns Hopkins Medical School. I'm sorry. Are you sure this is not the boat show? No, I have it. I do have it on me. I do. It's here. Thank you.

Ladies and gentlemen, distinguished faculty, administrators, friends and family and, of course, the graduating Class of 2003, I wish to say hello and thank you for bestowing this honor upon me as your Class Day speaker. After months of secret negotiations, several hundred secret ballots, and a weekend retreat with Vice President Dick Cheney in his secret mountain bunker, a Class Day speaker was chosen, and it was me. You obviously have made a grave error. But it's too late now. So let's just go with it.

Today's speech is going to be a little different, a little unorthodox. Some of you may find it to be shocking. I'm not going to stand up here and try to be funny. Because even though I am a professional comedian of the highest caliber, I've decided to do one thing that a lot of people are probably afraid to do, and that's give it to you straight.

As most of you are probably aware, I didn't graduate from Harvard. In fact, I never even got a call back from Admissions. Damn you, Harvard! Damn you! I told myself I would not get emotional today. But damn it, I'm here, and sometimes it's just good to cry.

I'm not one of you. Okay? I can't relate to who you are and what you've been through. I graduated from the University of Life. All right? I received a degree from the School of Hard Knocks. And our colors were black and blue, baby. I had office hours with the Dean of Bloody Noses. All right? I borrowed my class notes from Professor Knuckle Sandwich and his teaching assistant, Ms. Fat Lip Thon Nyun. That's the kind of school I went to for real, okay?

So my gift to you, Class of 2003, is to tell you about the real world through my eyes, through my experiences. And I'm sorry, but I refuse to sugarcoat it. I ain't gonna do it. And I probably shouldn't use the word "ain't" during this day in which we celebrate education. But that's just the way I play it, Homes.

Graduates, if you will indulge me for a moment, let me paint a picture of what it's like out there. The last four or, for some of you, five years you've been living in a fantasyland, running around, talking about Hemingway, or Clancy, or, I don't know, I mean whatever you read here at Harvard. The novelization of *The Matrix,* I don't know. I don't know what you do here.

But I do know this. You're about to enter into a world filled with hypocrisy and doublespeak, a world in which your limo to the airport is often a half hour late. In addition to not even being a limo at all; oftentimes it's a Lincoln Town Car. You're about to enter a world where you ask your new assistant, Jamie, to bring you a tall nonfat latte. And he comes back with a short soy cappuccino. Guess what, Jamie? You're fired. Not too hard to get right, my friend.

A world where your acting coach, Bob Leslie-Duncan—yes, the Bob Leslie-Duncan—tells you time and time again that you will never, ever be considered as a dramatic actor because you don't play things real, and are too over the top. Amazing! Simply amazing!

I'm sorry, graduates. But this is a world where you aren't allowed to use your cell phone in airplanes, during live theater, at the movies, at funerals, or even during your own elective surgery. Apparently, the Berlin Wall went back up, because we now live in Russia. I mean just try lighting up a cigar in a movie theater or paying for a dinner for twenty friends with an autograph. It ain't that easy. Strong words, I know. Tough talk. But more like tough love. Because this is where my faith in you guys comes into play, Harvard University's graduating Class of 2003, without a doubt, the finest, most talented group of sexual beings this great land has to offer.

Now I know I blew some of your minds with my depiction of what it's really like out there. But if anyone can handle the ups and downs of this crazy blue marble we call Planet Earth, it's you guys. As I stare out into this vast sea of shining faces, I see the best and brightest. Some of you will be captains of industry and business. Others of you will go on to great careers in medicine, law, and public service. Four of you—and I'm not at liberty to say which four—will go on to magnificent careers in the porno industry. I'm not trying to be funny. That's just a statistical fact.

One of you, specifically John Lee, will spend most of your time just hanging out in your car eating nachos. You will all come back from time to time to this beautiful campus for reunions, and ask the question, "Does anyone ever know what happened to John Lee?" At that point, he will invariably pop out from the bushes and yell, "Nachos anyone?" At first it will scare the crap out of you. But then you'll share a laugh with your classmates and ultimately look forward to John jumping out of the bushes as a yearly event.

I'd like to change gears here, if I could. Talk a little bit about *Saturday Night Live*. Now, during my eighteen-year stint on the show, I had the chance to play or impersonate some very interesting people, none more interesting than our current president, Mr. George W. Bush. Now in some cases, you actually have contact with some of the people you play. As a by-product of this former situation, the president and myself have become quite good friends. In fact, I might even call him a father figure of sorts, granted a dim-witted father figure who likes to take a lot of naps and start wars, but a father figure nonetheless.

When I told the president that I'd be speaking here today, he wondered if I would express some sentiments to you. And I said I'd do my best. So, if you don't mind, I'd like to read this message from the president of the United States.

Students, faculty, families, and distinguished guests, I just want to take time to congratulate you on your outstanding achievement as graduates of the Class of 2002. The great thing about being the Class of 2002 is that you can always remember what year you graduated because 2002 is a palindrome, which, of course, is a word or number that is the same read backwards or forwards. I'll bet you're surprised I know that word, but I do. So you can suck on it.

Make no mistake, Harvard University is one of the finest in the land. And its graduates are that fine as well. You're young men and women whose exuberance exude a confident confidence of a bygone era. I believe it was Shakespeare who said it best when he said, "Look yonder into the darkness for knowledge onto which I say go onto that which thou possess into thy night for thee have come with only a single sword and vanquished thee into darkness."

I'm going to be honest with you, I just made that up. But I don't know how to delete it from the computer. Tomorrow's graduation day speaker is former president of Mexico Ernesto Zedillo. Ernie's a good man, a deeply religious man, and one of the original members of the Latino boy band Menudo. So listen up to Ernie. He was at the beginning of the whole boy band explosion.

As you set off into the world, don't be afraid to question your leaders. But don't ask too many questions at one time or that are too hard, because your leaders get tired and/or cranky. All of you sitting here have the brightest of futures ahead. Many of you will go on to stellar careers and various pursuits. And four of you—and I'm not at liberty to say which four— will go on to star in the porno industry.

One of the challenges you will be faced with is finding a job in our depressed economy. In fact, the chances of landing a decent job are about as good as finding weapons of mass destruction in the Iraqi desert. Slim and none. And Slim just left the building. In fact, the closest thing I found to looking like a weapon of mass destruction is the turd that Dick Cheney left in the Oval Office toilet about an hour ago. Man, that thing is a WMD if I've ever seen one. On that note, God bless and happy graduation.

You know, I sincerely hope you enjoy this next chapter of your life, because it's really going to be great, as long as you pay your taxes. And don't just take a year off because you think Uncle Sam is snoozing at the wheel, because he will descend upon you like a hawk from hell. Let's just put it this way. After some past indiscretions with the IRS, my take-home pay last year was nine thousand dollars.

I figured I'd leave you today with a song, if you will. So, Jeff, if you could come up here. Jeff Heck, everyone. Please welcome one of your fellow graduates. Jeff is, of course, from Eliot House. You know what, you guys? You guys at Eliot House, give yourselves a nice round of applause because you had the head lice scare this year, and it shut you down for most of last semester. But you didn't mind the tents they set up for you, and you were just troupers. You really were.

Anyway, here's a song that I think really captures the essence of the Harvard experience. It goes a little like this. [SINGING] "Dust in the wind, all we are is dust in the wind."

Okay, you know what? I'm just realizing that this is a terrible graduation song. Once again, I'm sorry. This is the first time I've actually listened to the lyrics. Man, it's a downer. It's bleak.

Boy, I want to finish this. Just give me a minute, and let me figure out how to fix this thing. Okay. I think I got it. [SINGING]

Now don't hang on, nothing lasts forever but the
Harvard alumni endowment fund.
It adds up, has performed at 22 percent growth over
the last six years.

Dust in the wind, you're so much more than dust in the wind.
Dust in the wind, you're shiny little very smart pieces of dust in the wind.

Thank you. Good luck. And have a great day tomorrow.

The hilarious Will Ferrell is known for his impressions, his movies, and his work on Saturday Night Live, *for which he was nominated for an Emmy.*

AL FRANKEN

Harvard University, Class Day, 2002

I was all set to give a speech today entitled, "American Jihad." But after receiving several complaints, I've decided instead to give a less controversial speech entitled: "The Case for Profiling Young Arab Men."

Before I go any further, I would like to thank the university and President Summers for conferring upon me an honorary degree, an honorary doctorate, in Afro-American Studies. And especially for offering me a chair as a professor in that department—an offer I hereby most heartily accept.

I don't know much about Afro-American Studies. But I can assure you that I can use the summer to get myself up to speed.

But seriously, it is an honor to speak here today to you, the graduating Class of 2002, and to congratulate all of you—for getting into Harvard in the first place. Because let's face it, once you get in here, as long as you don't kill someone or embezzle one hundred thousand dollars from your student organization, you're going to graduate.

And to those of you who are graduating with honors: congratulations on doing some of the reading and on going to many of your classes, and getting notes from friends on the classes you didn't go to, and on handing in most of your papers on time. Way to go! Good work!

To those of you who did not graduate with honors, "Wow! Whoa!" But then again, congratulations on your hockey season.

As Jeremy [Bronson, who gave the Ivy Oration "Macroeconomic Theory in a Globally Integrated Economy"] said, most of you will be going out into the real world of law school, med school, or investment banking, and you will meet graduates from other colleges who had slightly better educations. Schools like Amherst, Haverford, Wesleyan, Ohio Wesleyan, and pretty much all the other Wesleyans.

But you will all have your Harvard degree. And you should never let others forget it!

There are ways to let people know you went to Harvard without just blurting out "I went to Harvard." First and foremost, remember—you didn't go to school in Boston, you went to school in Cambridge.

But if you really want to perfect the technique of slipping Harvard into a conversation, just consult your parents—they've been working on this from the moment you got your acceptance letter. My daughter is a junior here. Let me show you how I do it.

"Oh yeah, my daughter is twenty-one. She's a junior in college." (Please ask, please ask, please ask, please ask.) "Well, you know, it's great, because, you know, like, she's only really an hour from New York. And you know, we can take the shuttle up to visit her. We took the shuttle, actually, last week to Cambridge."

So, I went here. Class of '73. Graduated cum laude. In general studies. Harvard was in many ways a different place in those days. It was much whiter, much more male, and much more preppy. I remember the first person I met when I arrived. I had flown in from Minneapolis, taken a taxi directly to the Yard, and—lugging a duffel bag and an electric typewriter—found my freshman hall, Mower. And in the entryway was a guy wearing khakis and a polo shirt. He extended his hand in a very friendly manner—and this is an absolutely true story—and he said, "William Sutherland Strong. I'm from northern New Jersey, but my family moved from Massachusetts."

"When?" I asked.

"In the late eighteenth century."

Bill Strong and I became very good friends.

So, it was much preppier and much whiter. This disturbs some people. A while back Pat Buchanan said that Harvard should reserve 75 percent of its places for white Christians. As a Jew, I was offended, but looking around the Yard today at all the Asians, I kind of see what he's talking about. I mean they've got to stop admitting you people based on merit.

I spent three great years at Dunster House. One of the big changes in Harvard life has been the randomization of the housing process. In my day each house had its own distinctive character. Dunster House was known as the music-drug-theatre house. Mather House was known as the drug-jock house. Adams was the artsy-drug house, Mather House, as I said, was the drug-jock house. Quincy was also just the drug house. As were Leverett, Kirkland, Winthrop, and Lowell. Eliot was considered the preppy-drug house, but was also sometimes just thought of as the drug house. There was no quad, as such, back then, but people used to sneak up there to do drugs.

When I came to Harvard from Minnesota, I was a complete idiot. I remember freshman year thinking about becoming a visual studies major. And I needed to get into VES 40, which was the introductory course in visual studies, VES 40. And it was limited enrollment and you had to interview. And in the course catalogue it said VES 40, Carpenter Center, room whatever, Dr. J. (with a dot) Mendelsohn. So I go to the Carpenter Center and go to the room ready to impress Professor J. (dot) Mendelsohn, and the professor introduced herself to me. She says, "I'm Dr. Janet Mendelsohn." And I say, "Oh, I expected a man." So I didn't get into Visual Studies major and resigned myself to actually having to work for my degree.

I remember being in your place twenty-nine years ago, although I have to tell you I almost didn't graduate. My senior year I took a course, Soc Sci 134, "The Social History of the United States," taught by one of the university's most illustrious professors, Daniel Bell, who had coined the phrase "post-industrial society" and been on the cover of *Time* magazine. The problem was the class was at nine in the morning and that semester I was in a play at Dunster House—we really were the theater house—and rehearsals tended to go very late. I did manage to go to all the lectures, which were in William James, but the building, at least at that time, was very overheated, and I would routinely fall asleep in Professor Bell's lecture.

When the run of the play ended, we had a cast party which lasted through the entire night and I'm embarrassed to say I got a little drunk. And when 9 A.M. rolled around, having not slept, I for some reason thought it was a good idea to show up at Soc Sci 134 wearing a pajama top. I fell asleep and then at the end of the lecture, I stood up and I kind of passed out, falling into Dr. Bell's arms.

It occurred to me soon after that I might be in danger of flunking Soc Sci 134. And I needed to pass it in order to graduate. So I went to my TF [teaching fellow] and asked him what I needed to pass. And he told me that Dr. Bell thought I was a drug addict. So he suggested I talk to Bell and ask him what I could do to make sure I passed the course.

So I made an appointment with Dr. Bell for noon the next day. When I got to his office, he was meeting with a grad student, so his secretary asked me to go out into the lounge and wait for him, where I sat on the couch and immediately fell asleep. The next thing I saw was Dr. Bell leaning over me, saying, "Do you want to sleep or do you want to talk to me?"

I said, "Talk with you!" So we met in his office and I explained to him about the play and the rehearsals going late and the building being overheated, and Dr. Bell told me he felt it was a student's responsibility to stay conscious during class. Then he told me that the final exam—and the whole grade was based on the final exam, there were no papers, no quizzes, no tests, no midterms—the final exam was based solely on the reading. If I did all the reading, I'd be fine. So, I thanked him and went back to my room and looked at the reading list for the first time, and it was the longest reading list I'd ever seen at Harvard. No one could possibly do all this reading. So I spent the entire reading period in Lamont reading the reading list. And actually, it was great. The entire social history of our country unfolded before me there in Lamont. It was inspiring really, and it made me wish I had stayed awake for the lectures.

So, then on the way to the exam, it was in Sever, it occurred to me that maybe Bell was screwing with me. You know, why wouldn't he screw with a drug addict? I mean, what if the exam isn't on the reading? What if it's on the lectures? So I get into Sever and I get my blue book and I get the exam and I look at the first question, and it's directly from the reading. Second question, directly from the reading. They're all—everything on this exam—directly from the reading.

So a few days later I go to the TF's office to pick up my exam, and he says, "Bell's pissed. You got the highest grade of anyone in the entire class." It's a lecture of about 120 people. Of course. I was the only one who did all the reading. So now Bell thinks that a drug addict got the highest grade in his class. So I'm laughing until I remember that I took the course pass-fail.

To this day, I believe if I had gotten an A in Soc Sci 134 instead of a pass, my Stuart Smalley movie would have been a huge hit, and I'd be a big movie star today.

I want to take this moment to congratulate today's Ivy Orators, Taii Bullock and Jeremy Bronson, on your very funny remarks. You're terrific. Where are you? Taii? [APPLAUSE] I was, ironically, the Ivy Orator twenty-nine years ago. And I'm afraid I used the "f" word quite a few times in my speech. It was 1973. And a couple weeks later I received a note through the class marshal's office from an outraged parent, saying, "We came to watch you graduate from college, not from kindergarten." I've always felt kinda bad about that, and I was hoping to be invited back so that I could apologize.

Now, I know I wasn't the first choice to speak here this afternoon. I know this because the *Crimson* article announcing I'd be the Class Day speaker made a point of underscoring that fact many times. Allow me to quote from the front page of the *Harvard Crimson* of April 16:

Author and comedian Al Franken '73 will offer words of wisdom to graduating seniors on Class Day, senior class marshals announced yesterday. . . . Last year rock superstar Bono spoke to an audience of about

30,000—and some students hoped for a non-Harvard celebrity this year as well. "I'm disappointed it's not Madonna," said Dorothy Fortenberry '02. The list of favored candidates included Madonna, as well as Denzel Washington, Halle Berry, Robert DeNiro, Chris Rock, Jerry Seinfeld, and former New York City mayor Rudolf Guiliani. Franken was not on the initial list of candidates, but members of the Class Day Committee said he was not a last resort. "We went into this realizing that most people on the list are extremely busy and have hectic schedules," said Chad G. Callahan '02, first class vice president.

So, yes, I was available. Actually, I had to reschedule an audition for a voice-over for a hemorrhoid commercial, but it's not really worth getting into.

And I must say it's a little intimidating following Bono. In order to feel less intimidated, I'm simply telling myself that last year's speaker was Sonny Bono.

Actually, if you want to talk about intimidating, as was mentioned earlier, Mother Teresa was the Class Day speaker in 1982. But I read her speech, and I have to tell you, I don't think she was funny at all. "Sanctity of life"? Ha, ha. I'm sorry, Mother Teresa, but I don't get it. I'm not laughing.

So why me? Other than the availability issue? Well, if you think about it, in a way, I'm the perfect person to be up here dispensing advice. First of all, I am not a hopeless failure. There's no point in getting advice from hopeless failures.

On the other hand, enormous successes such as Bono and Mother Teresa have little to offer in the way of practical advice for ordinary people. Take Mother Teresa. Though I don't want it to seem like I'm beating up on her, I think you'd have to agree that Mother Teresa did not live a very balanced life. While what she did for the poor of Calcutta was commendable, she gave up a number of very important things, such as having a family and exploring sides to her personality other than just "the self-sacrificing living saint" side.

No, the perfect person to be speaking here today is me, someone who's had success, yet still knows what it's like not to be your first, second, third, or even eighth choice. So what can I tell you today? Well, I'm not going to try to pass off glib aphorisms as actual knowledge like so many commencement speakers do.

Take, for example, best-selling author Anna Quindlen, who at a commencement address a while back said this: "If you win the rat race, you're still a rat." It's cute, cute, but if you think about it, it's really nothing more than an all-purpose excuse not to succeed. My version of that quote goes, "If you win the rat race, you will never have trouble feeding your family."

For some reason, commencement speakers, almost all of whom have been selected because of their notable achievements, love to warn about the fraudulence of success. This spring countless graduates of other universities have been told, "It's lonely at the top." It's not. Believe me. It's much, much lonelier at the bottom.

Here's another soothing but useless bromide: "Every time one door closes, another door opens." That's not true. And very often when one door closes, another does open: A trapdoor leading directly to that lonely place at the bottom.

And no doubt on some campus somewhere proud parents who never made more than twelve thousand dollars a year had to listen to Donald Trump tell them that failure is a better teacher than success.

Here's a line from late Massachusetts senator Paul Tsongas that is often quoted at commencements: "No man on his deathbed ever said, 'I wish I had spent more time at the office.'" How does he know that? I'll bet someone on their deathbed said, "I wish I had spent more time at the office in my twenties and thirties; I would have had a much better life." Gurgle—dead. I'm sure that happens. And it's quite possible that some former Enron or Arthur Andersen executive will use his last breath to say, "I wish I had spent more time at the office and less time in prison."

Take risks, sure. And don't be paralyzed by fear, especially by fear of failure. At least not until you're thirty. Twenty-nine years ago, I left here in a '65 Buick Le Sabre with enough gas money to get to Los Angeles, where I did stand-up comedy with my partner Tom Davis. After two years of struggle, playing dives and taking humiliating odd jobs, Tom and I were hired by Lorne Michaels to write for a new late-night comedy show called *Saturday Night Live.* We were the only writers hired whom Lorne hadn't met. To this day, we believe that had he met us, we never would have been hired.

Since those first glory days of *Saturday Night Live,* I've had my successes and I've had my failures, and I have to tell you, the successes have been more fun. But what has sustained me through all of it were the people closest to me: my parents, my wife, and my kids.

I have been married for twenty-six years. And I honestly believe I love my wife more right now than I did on our wedding day. But I know for sure that I love her more now than I did fifteen years ago, when we couldn't stand each other.

Every marriage goes through a difficult phase. Anyone who tells you otherwise is either lying to you, lying to themselves, or is married to someone really fabulous.

But we were lucky. My wife shaped up, and we stayed together. And I'm proud to say that I think I have two very "together" kids. This is despite the fact that my son spends hours a day playing a video game called *Grand Theft Auto III,* in which the object is to pick up a prostitute in a stolen car and rape and murder her.

My daughter is a junior here at Harvard. And I don't know if I mentioned that. No, my daughter goes to Harvard. She does. And she's on track to graduate with honors.

Parenting is the hardest job you'll ever love. First and foremost, being a good parent means spending lots of time with your children. I personally hate the phrase "Quality Time." Kids don't want Quality Time, they want Quantity Time, big, stinking, lazy, nonproductive Quantity Time. On the other hand, it's important for every parent to maintain balance in his or her life. Don't be a slave to your child. No one respects a slave—unless he's played by Morgan Freeman.

Next year I plan to be seated where you are, a proud parent, next to my beautiful daughter Thomasin, listening, hopefully, to Madonna. All of you who are graduating today are here because of your parents. In many cases your parents have made tremendous sacrifices so that you were able to go to Harvard. Whether it be taking an extra job to pay for tuition, or simply spending hours helping you with your homework when you were younger. Or maybe their sacrifice was in the form of paying for a round-the-clock SAT tutor. Or perhaps they just wrote a huge check to Harvard so that you could get in. You know who you are and the rest of us hate you.

So, what do we, the parents, expect of you? Well, it would be nice if you had a clearly defined career goal that we could easily explain to our friends. But most of all what we want from you is gratitude. Simple gratitude. And so today, I'd just like to conclude my remarks by asking the graduates here to take a moment to thank your parents.

I want you all to turn to your parents and say, "Thanks, Mom and Dad, I love you," or "Thanks, Mom and Stepdad and Dad and Stepmom or . . ." You get the idea. And then I want you to hug them and kiss them. Go ahead. Don't mind me.

[EVERYONE HUGS, ETC.]

Thank you.

So, congratulations, graduates. Congratulations, parents, friends, and relatives. Oh, yeah, "Go forth unafraid!"

Best-selling author Al Franken is a liberal satirist and a graduate of Saturday Night Live. *He has won five Emmys for his television work.*

MUSICIANS

Without music to decorate it, time is just a bunch of boring production deadlines or dates by which bills must be paid.

—*Frank Zappa*

RENÉE FLEMING

When asked to give this address, I immediately said yes, because I possess that mutant gene that compels me to agree to absolutely everything I find terrifying. I suspect some of you have that gene too, or you wouldn't be here at this wonderful institution. So I've agreed to the responsibility of summarizing your Juilliard education, while inspiring you to glorious futures in ten minutes or less—terrifying indeed. But then I took a poll, and not a single friend could remember who spoke at their graduation, which increased my confidence dramatically.

What on earth could I say, since I honestly don't feel very different from you or removed from my graduation? My search for a purpose, feelings of confusion, hope, and ambition still make up a major part of every day. But then I stopped thinking about me—not easy for a singer—and began thinking about you. You are extraordinary, courageous, beautiful, and historically unique as a graduating class.

Think about your Juilliard experience. In the middle of 1999, your freshman year, you joined the world in a giddy, exhilarating millennium celebration—a fever when we all, even those of us old enough to know better, imagined that the next century would be different.

Then in 2001, the beginning of your junior year, you witnessed our young city's loss of innocence in September just as

49

you began your studies. Those weeks made me question my very worth as a musician, as I rehearsed *Otello* in Chicago, and made me ask questions about my function and purpose in society. And as you graduate today, with Afghanistan and Iraq, the world has transformed into a more uncertain place than when you began here. You have not only gained mastery of your disciplines and instruments these past four years, but have experienced a lifetime of joy and sorrow. So you and I are very different. When I graduated, I suffered primarily from the gnawing fear that I would never once approximate something as glorious as Leontyne Price's high C no matter how much I practiced. I was equally concerned about whether or not the quality of pizza would be as high at my next destination. I've since given up on Leontyne's high C, and fully boned corsets do not allow for much leeway on the pizza front, sadly.

So, while you're standing in the grocery line holding Spam instead of foie gras for a few years, ponder the following: Those of you who perform—musicians and dancers—will have by now practiced perhaps three thousand hours a year, times fifteen years, which equals forty-five thousand hours. Which means collectively that you as a group will have practiced 11 million hours. The tyranny of performing is that the drive is unrelenting and inflexible. It's never good enough; our critics don't even begin to know how inept and awful we feel we are, how undeserving of success, the torture of a constant striving for perfection for actors, historians, composers, writers, choreographers, musicologists, and more—all of you called to the arts, to creativity, and to self-expression.

What to do with this extraordinary legacy of experience you've had in four years? You're already primed to "make a difference," to begin your lives with one foot rooted in eternity, because your experience has aged you more than you can imagine. Civilizations are judged on their wars and their arts; that's the measure that's taken. How do we want to be judged? Here are just five ideas:

Lead. You are artists—keepers of the human spirit and our noblest thoughts and feelings. Throughout time, Art has proven to be the highest expression of mankind while History has consistently proven to be the opposite—greed, hatred, and lust for power. Be history's Greek chorus. As Homer's King says to the tearful Odysseus regarding the fall of Troy: "The gods arranged all this, and sent them their misfortunes in order that future generations might have something to sing about." Often, what man does is base. What we have to say about it after the fact—and hopefully before—is inspirational.

Be resilient. If you find that your chosen dream becomes unattainable, there are many types of success. ChevronTexaco has just announced the end of its sponsorship of the live-from-the-Met radio broadcasts. Six orchestras have closed this season, and a few others are on the way. The greatest service you can provide for the arts in this country is finding an audience for your colleagues. Recent decades have seen tremendous growth in performance organizations, conservatories producing wonderfully trained artists, all dressed up with less and less of a public to perform for. The recent Pew Charitable Trust study called for a profound policy shift from strengthening the supply of artists to stimulating the public's demand for the arts. The Trust report further reports that your generation will be solving these problems. Challenge the idea that the arts are for a select few—teach, make more people love what you love, and help them to understand why you dedicated those 11 million hours in the first place.

Be creative. Please give our citizens an alternative to television (and especially reality TV) as a substitute for anything resembling the creative process. Help them to think more, experience more, and live vicariously less. Be creative in your own lives every day—it feeds the soul. Even those of us who perform are fed by our imaginations. I am always humbled by spontaneous inspiration, that moment on stage when something new occurs to me and, thanks to the now more than forty-five thousand hours of practice, I have the courage to try it. I never, ever feel more alive than in that moment.

See humor in as many things as possible. After a recent benefit concert, a breathless couple pressed a gift into my palm. Earplugs. They proclaimed with enormous enthusiasm that they came to the concert armed with earplugs because they hate concerts with singers but came to support the cause. Wonder of wonders, they never used the earplugs. I said, "That's the most wonderful backhanded compliment I've ever received." Let's face it: In how many fields could one have such unconventional praise?

Stay balanced. If I knew then what I know now, I would have had a lot more fun while I was worrying about how I was going to claw my way to the top (not that I was ambitious, mind you). My favorite tempering statement is: On my deathbed, what choice would I wish to have made now? Your life is a series of choices, and you may find yourself standing at this podium one day, as I am, wondering if you made the right ones.

Always be a student. You think you've graduated—but this is just the beginning. Not long ago, bored at a spa (or escaping exercise), I saw a psychic and I asked her about my beloved Juilliard voice teacher, Beverley Johnson. Without skipping a beat, she said, "Oh, she's learning a great deal, studying with scholars." I don't know if it's true, but it really sounds like her. I still see every engagement as an opportunity to learn something new, and I hope I always will.

We have chosen a rare and privileged profession, one which actually encourages our uniqueness. In the words of Martha Graham: "There is no satisfaction whatever at any time. There is only a queer, divine dissatisfaction: a blessed unrest that keeps us marching and makes us more alive than the rest."

I want to tell you a story. I was asked to sing "Amazing Grace" at Ground Zero. Faced with thousands of people whose loss was so profound—a sea of grief—I didn't know how I could sing. I couldn't look at the faces, once I began. It wasn't until sometime later that I had the realization about why I was there: to bring music, to comfort and provide solace for these people.

Please, remember your legacy of experience. You are extraordinary—historically unique as a graduating class—and we need you to be courageous.

American soprano Renée Fleming has enjoyed success across a range of musical styles, from the stages of opera houses worldwide to her award-winning recordings.

BILLY JOEL

Berklee College of Music, 1993

Thank you, President Berk, trustees, faculty, staff and students of Berklee, guests, and Johnny Mandel, who is also being honored here today.

I understand that there are over five hundred students in this graduating class. What an amazing thing. When I was a young musician, the only option available to pursue secondary education in music was to attend a classical conservatory. Obviously, I didn't choose that route, and although the one I ended up taking has been rather circuitous, I am truly pleased that the road has twisted and turned its way up the East Coast to Boston. The Berklee College of Music represents the finest contemporary music school there is, and I am honored to be here with you this morning to celebrate the 1993 commencement.

I have been asked many times, "Why do musicians give so much time to charitable causes?" I know a few musicians who are motivated by pure guilt—the result of a dissolute and misspent youth combined with the onset of remorse and middle age. I am not as remote from these few as I would like to think. Some are motivated to activism by a sincere idealism, which musicians and artists in general must have in spades to be able to deal with the disappointments and cynicism we all encounter in what seems an often endlessly futile labor of love. Perhaps it is mainly because musicians want to be the loud voice for so many quiet hearts.

Maybe it's because we know what it is like to be completely alone, to be unemployed, to have to struggle. Historically, musicians know what it is like to be outside the norm—walking the high wire without a safety net. Our experience is not so different from those who march to the beat of different drummers. We experience similar difficulties, weakness, failures, and sadness, but we also celebrate the joys and successes—these are the things that we translate and express in music.

And still, we hear the same question: So when are you going to get a real job? How many times have you been asked this question or some incarnation thereof? Beethoven heard it. John Lennon heard it. Milli Vanilli heard it. Bob Marley heard it. Janis Joplin heard it. Tchaikovsky heard it. Charlie Parker heard it, Verdi, Debussy. When I was nineteen, I made my first good week's pay as a club musician. It was enough money for me to quit my job at the factory and still pay the rent and buy some food. I freaked. I ran home and tore off my clothes and jumped around my tiny little apartment shouting, "I'm a musician, I'm a musician!" It was one of the greatest days of my life, just to be able to make a living as a musician alone, to earn money doing what I loved to do.

Artists—musicians, painters, writers, poets—always seem to have had the most accurate perception of what is really going on around them, not the official version or the popular perception of contemporary life. When I look at great works of art or listen to inspired music, I sense intimate portraits of the specific times in which they were created. And they have lasted because someone, somewhere felt compelled to create it, and someone else understood what they were trying to do. Why do we still respond when we hear the opening notes of Beethoven's Fifth Symphony—DA DA DA DA? Or Gershwin's *Rhapsody in Blue*? Or Little Richard's "Tutti Frutti"? Because when we hear it, we realize that we are still bound by a common emotion to those who came before us. Like family, we are irrevocably tied to each other because that same emotion still exists today. This is what all good musicians understand.

I can't think of one person I've ever met who didn't like some type of music. More than art, more than literature, music is universally accessible. For whatever reason, not all people are born with the particular gift that we have: the gift of being able to express ourselves through music. And, believe me, it is a gift. But people who don't have this ability still need to find a way to give a voice to what they're thinking and feeling, to find something that connects them with others. As human beings, we need to know that we are not alone, that we are not crazy or that we are all completely out of our minds, that there are other people out there who feel as we do, who live as we do, who love as we do, who are like us.

Music does this in such a complete and uncomplicated way. There is great magic in this. In a way, we are magicians. We are alchemists, sorcerers, and wizards. We are a very strange bunch. But there is great fun in being a wizard. And great power, too.

Nowadays, we are living in a time when American popular music is finally being recognized as one of our most successful exports. The demand is huge. The whole world loves American movies, blue jeans, jazz, and rock and roll. And it is probably a better way to get to know our country than by what the politicians or airline commercials represent. Musicians now find themselves in the unlikely position of being legitimate. At least the IRS thinks so. Once they discovered that we were actually capable of making "money," the free ride was over. No one eludes Uncle Sam's tax man anymore like they did in the old days when we were outlaws, hippies, beatniks and weirdos and—the most shadowy group of all—jazz players! No, we're all corporations and contractors and production companies now—and by the way, I hope most of you have taken some basic accounting courses and have a lawyer in the family. You're going to need both.

So why do musicians give so much time to charitable causes? There are many reasons, but the most humanitarian cause that we can give our time to is the creation and performance of music itself. That is the gift we have been given, that is our destiny and our usefulness as human beings in the short time we have in this world. And that's plenty of reason.

And I hope you don't make music for some vast, unseen audience or market or ratings share or even for something as tangible as money. For though it's crucial to make a living, that shouldn't be your inspiration or your aspiration. Do it for yourself, your highest self, for your own pride, joy, ego, gratification, expression, love, fulfillment, happiness—whatever you want to call it. Do it because it's what you have to do. And if you make this music for the human needs you have within yourself, then you do it for all humans who need the same things. Ultimately, you enrich humanity with the profound expression of these feelings.

Now, I have been both praised and criticized in my time. The criticism stung, but the praise sometimes bothered me even more. To have received such praise and honors like this has always been puzzling to me when I consider myself to be an inept pianist, a bad singer, and a merely competent songwriter. What I do, in my opinion, is by no means extraordinary. I am, as I've said, merely competent. But in an age of incompetence, that makes me extraordinary. Maybe that's why I've been able to last in this crazy business. I actually know how to play my ax and write a song. That's my job.

So when are you going to get a real job? When are you going to get serious about life? I have news for them: When are you going to get a real job? This is a real job—as real as a doctor, a teacher, or a scientist and just as important as and very similar to healing, teaching, and inventing. But even more fun because we have that wizard and sorcerer bit going for us. I have said before to those who have expressed doubts and misgivings about their ability to live this kind of life, maybe they shouldn't try, because being a musician is not something you choose to be, it is something you are, like tall or short or straight or gay. There is no choice, either you is or you ain't.

Now, I'm sure it must be daunting to graduate in times of financial distress and unemployment. But consider this: Have you listened to the radio lately? Have you heard the canned, frozen, and processed product being dished up to the world as American popular music today? What an incredible opportunity for a new movement of American composers and musicians to shape what we will be listening to in the years to come. While most people are satisfied with the junk food being sold as music, you have the chance and the responsibility to show us what a real banquet music can be. You have learned the fine art of our native cuisine—blues, jazz, gospel, Broadway, rock and roll, and pop. After all this schooling, you should know how to cook! So cook away and give us the good stuff for a change. Please. We need it. We need it very, very much. Congratulations and good luck!

Over the past thirty years, "Piano Man" Billy Joel has racked up an impressive number of multiplatinum albums and hit singles.

YOKO ONO

Maine College of Art, 2003

rt is Love.

What we, artists, give to the society is love. Right now, love is what is most needed in our society. Love comes from our heart. It is not something we can manufacture. Each artwork is an extension of our heartbeat, our life force, and a miracle to be shared with the world.

One day, after September 11, I happened to be at an art fair and was surprised that I loved everything that was there. Every artwork, down to a painting of a clown . . . which, I must say, I used to deplore. Suddenly, I had so much love for every artist who was behind those works. I felt like hugging each one of them. The fact that they were painting these paintings instead of doing something else like arguing, fighting, or killing made me feel so thankful to them. *What's wrong with a clown painting,* I said to myself. *Thank you for doing this. It's beautiful!*

Art is a way of survival.

During World War II, St. Petersburg was surrounded by the German army and cut off from Moscow for months. Finally there was no food, no heat, just the sound of German bombings. The radio DJ tried to cheer people up by playing music, talking, and cracking jokes. Eventually, he also became too tired to keep the show going and just let a metronome tick live on the radio. People no more had the strength to do anything but lie down and listen and hold on to that sound of a metronome ticking through day and night. That's how they kept their sanity and survived. That DJ, I think, was a true artist.

Let me tell you my experience in Japan. During the war, I was sent to a remote village with my younger brother and sister. One day I felt very bad that my brother was looking depressed. He was a bubbly, cute kid who was always laughing. Now the laughing stopped. I knew it was because we didn't have anything to eat. So I told him that we were going to play a game and dream up a hefty dinner menu. "I want ice cream," he said, after thinking for a while. I told him that we have to start with a soup and a main course. We created an elaborate menu in the air. Pretty soon, my brother gave the sweet chuckle I was longing to hear.

Art surpasses all conventions.

George Bernard Shaw said to Sarah Bernhardt, the most celebrated actress of the day, "In a play, the script is everything, all an actress has to do is to follow the script." You can say that he was an early male chauvinist, or a playwright with pride, or both. To prove him wrong, Sarah Bernhardt promptly did a performance reading nothing but phone numbers from a phone book and touched people's hearts so much that they all cried. I wasn't there, so I don't know if this incredible thing really happened or not. But, nevertheless, I told this anecdote to John, my husband, and grabbed a newspaper that was lying around there, to prove . . . I don't know what . . . to prove something. John promptly turned the tape recorder on and joined me with his guitar. That really did happen. It became an ad-lib performance called "No Bed for Beatle John" and is on our record "Unfinished Music Number Two: Life with the Lions." I'm sure Sarah never imagined she would be inspiring an Asian woman artist so many decades later.

Art is not planning. It's an attitude of using a situation that's given to you. It's called a blessing, and it grows in a much higher dimension than what we miserable mortals plan to do.

It was lunchtime in London, 1966, and I was getting hungry while I was checking on my art pieces in Indica Gallery, where I had my show. One of the frequent visitors to the show told me that he would treat me to lunch. We went to the corner sandwich place. While I was eating my sandwich, he told me that he could give me the money to make a feature-length film, if I had an idea for it. I immediately raised my hand, because my mouth was full with a bite of the sandwich. "I got an idea!" I said it like I thought the offer would disappear unless I had the idea right away. My idea was to make a feature-length film of the short "Bottoms" film I made in New York City. I told the guy that I did make a short of it in New York. I thought it was so hilarious not only to make a "Bottoms" film, but to simply repeat the performance and make a feature film of it. How dumb can it get? It was my piece de resistance to intellec-tualism! Surprisingly, the guy said, "Okay. That sounds interesting." So I immediately started making the film. I got outdated rolls of film that people were going to throw out, borrowed a camera from a friend, and made the film in the living room of a friend's house, which was offered to me for the filming. A film editing house gave me free usage of the editing equipment after midnight, when nobody was using it.

The "Bottoms" film became such a sensation even before it was released, the guy who had originally said he would put up the money called me and said I was getting too popular, and he changed his mind. So he did not give me the money after all. That became a bit hard for me, because I was counting on it. But without his first suggestion, I would never have thought of making the film. So he was, after all, an angel. My work was helped by countless angels in my life. Of course, you will be helped too. Just recognize where the angel is coming from. It is never from a predictable place.

Art is not about creating. . . . It's about being creative in changing the value of our lives.

Negativity is constantly trying to slip into our lives. We get depressed about it. Don't be depressed or be scared. Don't close your eyes to it. Use it as a fertilizer to be creative. Art is to make it easier for us to dance through life.

Marianne Williamson said: "Our deepest fear is that we are powerful beyond measure. It is our light, not our darkness, that most frightens us."

Mother Teresa said: "Give the world the best you have and you may get kicked in the teeth. Give the world the best you have anyway."

I say: You can't dance if you've got too much muck in your head. Let it go. Be free, and dance through life. After all, in the big picture, we are all just a part of the harmony called the universe. Remember love. Remember our hearts are one. Even when we are fighting with each other, our hearts are beating in unison. I love you.

Yoko Ono, who has been blamed for the breakup of the Beatles, was known as an artist and musician before she met John Lennon. Since his death, she has continued to make her mark in international art and music circles.

STING

Berklee College of Music, 1994

So I'm standing here in a strange hat and a strange, flowing gown in front of what looks very much like an audience, and I'm about to do something that I don't do very often, which is to make speeches in public. And I'm asking myself how I managed to end up here.

This was never in any plan I'd outlined for myself. Nevertheless, I'm here, and you're all expecting something coherent, and perhaps meaningful, to come out of my mouth. I'll try, but there are no guarantees. And I have to say I'm a little bit nervous. You might think this is strange for a man who makes his living playing in stadiums, but I often stand in the middle of a stadium full of people and ask myself the same question, "How the hell did I end up here?" The simple answer is I'm a musician. And for some reason I've never had any other ambition but to be a musician. So by way of explanation, I'll start at the beginning.

My earliest memory is also my earliest musical memory. I remember sitting at my mother's feet as she played the piano. She always played tangos, for some reason. Perhaps it was the fashion at the time, I don't know. The piano was an upright with worn brass pedals. And when my mother played one of her tangos, she seemed to become transported to another world. Her feet rocking rhythmically between the loud and soft pedals, her arms pumping to the odd rhythms of the tango, her eyes intent upon the sheet music in front of her.

For my mother, playing the piano was the only time that I wasn't the center of her world—the only time she ignored me. So I knew that something significant—some important ritual— was being enacted here. I suppose I was being initiated into something—initiated into some sort of mystery. The mystery of music.

And so I began to aspire to the piano and would spend hours hammering away at atonal clusters in the delusion that if I persisted long enough, my noise would become music. I still labor under this delusion. My mother cursed me with the fine ear of a musician but the hands of a plumber. Anyway, the piano had to be sold to help us out of a financial hole, and my career as an atonal serialist was mercifully stunted. It wasn't until an uncle of mine emigrated to Canada, leaving behind an old Spanish guitar with five rusty strings, that my enormous and clumsy fingers found a musical home, and I found what was to become my best friend. Where the piano had seemed incomprehensible, I was able to make music on the guitar almost instantaneously.

Melodies, chords, song structures fell at my fingertips. Somehow I could listen to a song on the radio and then make a passable attempt at playing it. It was a miracle. I spent hour after hour, day after day, month after month, just playing, rejoicing in the miracle and probably driving my parents round the bend.

But it was their fault in the first place. Music is an addiction, a religion, and a disease. There is no cure. No antidote. I was hooked.

There was only one radio station in England at that time— the BBC. And you could hear the Beatles and the Rolling Stones side by side with bits of Mozart, Beethoven, Glenn Miller, and even the blues. This was my musical education, its eclecticism supplemented by my parents' record collection of Rodgers and Hammerstein, Lerner and Lowe, Elvis Presley, Little Richard, and Jerry Lee Lewis. But it wasn't until the Beatles that I realized that perhaps I could make a living out of music.

The Beatles came from the same working-class background as I did. They were English, and Liverpool wasn't any fancier or more romantic than my own hometown. And my guitar went from being the companion of my solitude to the means of my escape.

There's a lot been written about my life after that time, so that I can't remember what's true and what isn't. I had no formal musical education. But I suppose I became successful by a combination of dumb luck, low cunning, and risk-taking born out of curiosity. I still operate in the same way. But your curiosity in music is never entirely satisfied. You could fill libraries with what I don't know about music. There's always something more to learn.

Now, musicians aren't particularly good role models in society. We really don't have a very good reputation. Philanderers, alcoholics, addicts, alimony-jumpers, tax-evaders. And I'm not just talking about rock musicians. Classical musicians have just as bad a reputation. And jazz musicians . . . forget it! But when you watch a musician play—when he enters that private musical world—you often see a child at play, innocent and curious, full of wonder at what can only be adequately described as a mystery—a sacred mystery even. Something deep. Something strange. Both joyous and sad. Something impossible to explain in words. I mean, what could possibly keep us playing scales and arpeggios hour after hour, day after year after year? Is it some vague promise of glory, money, or fame? Or is it something deeper?

Our instruments connect us to this mystery and a musician will maintain this sense of wonder till the day he or she dies. I had the privilege of spending some time with the great arranger Gil Evans in the last year of his life. He was still listening, still open to new ideas, still open to the wonder of music. Still a curious child.

So we stand here in our robes with our diplomas, our degrees of excellence. Some are merely honorary, some diligently worked for. We have mastered the laws of harmony and the rules of counterpoint, the skills of arranging and orchestrating, of developing themes and rhythmic motifs. But do any of us really know what music is? Is it merely physics? Mathematics? The stuff of romance? Commerce? Why is it so important to us? What is its essence?

I can't even pretend to know. I've written hundreds of songs, had them published, had them in the charts, Grammys, and enough written proof that I'm a bona fide, successful songwriter. Still, if somebody asks me how I write songs, I have to say, "I don't really know." I don't really know where they come from. A melody is always a gift from somewhere else. You just have to learn to be grateful and pray that you will be blessed again some other time. It's the same with the lyrics. You can't write a song without a metaphor. You can mechanically construct verses, choruses, bridges, middle eights, but without a central metaphor, you ain't got nothing.

I often wonder: Where do melodies and metaphors come from? If you could buy them in a store I'd be first in the queue, believe me. I spend most of my time searching for these mysterious commodities, searching for inspiration.

Paradoxically, I'm coming to believe in the importance of silence in music. The power of silence after a phrase of music, for example; the dramatic silence after the first four notes of

Beethoven's Fifth Symphony, or the space between the notes of a Miles Davis solo. There is something very specific about a rest in music. You take your foot off the pedal and pay attention. I'm wondering whether, as musicians, the most important thing we do is merely to provide a frame for silence. I'm wondering if silence itself is perhaps the mystery at the heart of music. And is silence the most perfect music of all?

Songwriting is the only form of meditation that I know. And it is only in silence that the gifts of melody and metaphor are offered. To people in the modern world, true silence is something we rarely experience. It is almost as if we conspire to avoid it. Three minutes of silence seems like a very long time. It forces us to pay attention to ideas and emotions that we rarely make any time for. There are some people who find this awkward, or even frightening.

Silence is disturbing. It is disturbing because it is the wavelength of the soul. If we leave no space in our music—and I'm as guilty as anyone else in this regard—then we rob the sound we make of a defining context. It is often music born from anxiety to create more anxiety. It's as if we're afraid of leaving space. Great music's as much about the space between the notes as it is about the notes themselves. A bar's rest is as important and significant as the bar of demisemiquavers that precedes it. What I'm trying to say here is that if ever I'm asked if I'm religious, I always reply, "Yes, I'm a devout musician." Music puts me in touch with something beyond the intellect, something otherworldly, something sacred.

How is it that some music can move us to tears? Why is some music indescribably beautiful? I never tire of hearing Samuel Barber's Adagio for Strings or Fauré's Pavane or Otis Redding's "Dock of the Bay." These pieces speak to me in the only religious language I understand. They induce in me a state of deep meditation, of wonder. They make me silent.

It's very hard to talk about music in words. Words are superfluous to the abstract power of music. We can fashion words into poetry so that they are understood the way music is understood, but they only aspire to the condition where music already exists.

Music is probably the oldest religious rite. Our ancestors used melody and rhythm to co-opt the spirit world to their purposes—to try and make sense of the universe. The first priests were probably musicians, the first prayers probably songs.

So what I'm getting round to saying is that as musicians, whether we're successful, playing to thousands of people every night, or not so successful, playing in bars or small clubs, or not successful at all, just playing alone in your apartment to the cat, we are doing something that can heal souls, that can mend us when our spirits are broken.

Whether you make a million dollars or not one cent, music and silence are priceless gifts; may you always possess them. May they always possess you.

Sting, veteran of the well-known rock trio The Police, has enjoyed a successful solo music career since the mid-1980s and is also an environmental activist.

POETS

A poet's work is to name the unnameable, to point at frauds, to take sides, start arguments, shape the world, and stop it going to sleep.

—*Salman Rushdie*

MARVIN BELL

Dark Matter & Sticky Stuff

President Edmondson, distinguished trustees, members of the faculty, administration and staff, family and friends of the graduates, and members of the Class of 2002:

I am honored to have this opportunity to address the Class of 2002. I am here to say hello and good-bye. The good-bye comes first. For this is the day when you seniors say farewell. You say so long to the place where you learned, more than ever before, to live on your own and to think for yourself. Here you cultivated your social lives but also a sense of yourselves alone. The poet Rainer Maria Rilke speaks of a solitude that we carry with us, even in the midst of crowds. Here at Alfred you acquired both a greater knowledge of society and a better feeling for your insides.

Universities like Alfred exist because we have the language with which to teach and test you about many things, and wherever you go next, others will continue to test you about those things. But there are no exact words for what you learned here about your insides, and the tests for that are wholly of your own making.

You know, some of the friendships you made here will likely continue without a break, or, as has happened for me, return to you years later. Those friendships will carry a special emotional resonance. It always feels as if friends we made in high school and college know us better than friends we made later. Why is that? It's because we come to college raw. With raw insides. Don't forget, a college freshman is just a high school senior with two months' vacation. That was you, four years ago, but today you are a different person.

I remember those early feelings on campus. I came to study at Alfred in 1954. I came here from eastern Long Island, where even today there are people who live their entire lives fifty or seventy miles from New York City and never once go into the Big Apple. And we didn't look at maps. But I knew that Alfred was somewhere west of the City, and on Orientation Day I set out driving, thinking it was just the other side of the Hudson. Actually, Alfred was four hundred miles from my home. I would go into taverns along Route 17 and ask, "Can you tell me where Alfred is?" And the patrons in the bars would tell me, in one way or another, to keep moving. Of course, eventually I reached Alfred. I knew I was in Alfred because I arrived on campus on the twelfth of September and on the fourteenth, it snowed. In those years, it snowed all the time except during the Great Thaw, which occurred annually during Winter Carnival week when we needed snow to make ice sculptures.

The fifties were a time when one could offend others awfully easily. We cared perhaps too much about what others thought of us. And so Alfred was a revelation, because most of the professors and some of my fellow students were quite different from the people I knew in my small hometown. Professors, of course, are always different. That's what makes them so easy to imitate at parties. But there were students here too who had a passion for their work, whether it was studies or art or extracurricular projects, and I saw that it defined them. It wasn't the opinions of others that defined them as much as their personal goals and the thrill of pursuing their passions.

The Hungarian/Transylvanian-born psychologist, Mihaly Csikszentmihalyi, writes of a concept he calls "flow." Flow is the state you enter—he calls it "optimal experience"—when you are so completely involved in what you are doing that you lose track of time. You feel serene, sometimes ecstatic. You have a sense of clarity. You transcend your ego. Whatever you are doing, doing it is its own reward. You've all had this experience, whether you were enthralled by art or science or sports or, on the other side of joy, cramming the night before an exam. That's how it is for me when I write poetry late at night. It's midnight, and suddenly it's five A.M. Where did the time go? In a sense, a person who has an all-consuming passion escapes time. We say about people with a passion that they "lose themselves" in their work. Which really means, in another sense, that they *find* themselves in their work. Those students with work to do were way ahead of me. They were already thinking for themselves, they were replacing that inhibiting, smoldering self-consciousness I felt as a freshman with the self-awareness of a graduate.

So we come to college raw, and while we are engaged in the life of the mind, a lot of other stuff is happening inside us, perceptions and emotions for which there are no ready words. To express how life feels, we have to go by way of dream images, song lyrics and all kinds of music, dance and mime, painting and sculpture, fiction and poetry. There are no words for feelings because words are words and feelings are feelings. All art is, first of all, an expression of what life feels like.

And it isn't just in the arts that we have to look for new words. Have you ever heard the terms "dark matter" and "sticky stuff"? If they sound to you as if they refer to things we can't see and can't shake, you have it right. Yet these are in fact scientific terms—"dark matter" and "sticky stuff"—terms used in astronomy and quantum physics.

I like ideas to have a little dirt on their shoes. So I was downright giddy when the astronomers came up with the term "dark matter" to refer to what they *can't* see that lies between what they *can* see. In other words, dark matter is the stuff between the stuff. Meanwhile, the quantum physicists decided to refer to what holds together the smallest recordable elements of the atom as—what else?—"sticky stuff."

What terrific terms for the unknown that is all about us. I may not be able to follow Einstein's Theory of Relativity, but I feel I understand in my bones the concepts of "dark matter" and "sticky stuff." I have not traveled in outer space, I do not leave my body, I have never—not even once—been abducted by aliens, I am neither a psychic nor a seer, but I have been living with dark matter and sticky stuff my whole life.

Think about it. Philosophy and religion are about . . . dark matter and sticky stuff. Morality and ethics are certainly about dark matter and sticky stuff. How about psychology and therapy? How about history, for that matter? Some of the time, simply trying to get the facts straight is a struggle with dark matter and sticky stuff.

Now I need to insert a small qualification here. My wife, Dorothy, who is here today, has cautioned me about applying the concepts of dark matter and sticky stuff too widely. She points out, for example, that I should probably not apply them to gourmet cooking, although, being a known chocoholic, she says she will permit me to apply the terms to desserts. "Waiter, I'll have the dark matter, and she'll have that sticky stuff."

Incidentally, recently the astronomers learned that there is even more Dark Matter in the heavens than they thought.

Robotic telescopes have now mapped the region of the universe inhabited by Earth, and the astronomers have found that cosmic structures have a maximum size. They weren't sure about this before, but now they know that these structures can be only so big. And once again, they have come up with a remarkable term. This limit, this maximum size, they call—get this—"the end of greatness." We short people are not that happy to have a lack of size equated with the end of greatness, but okay.

Well, we know how to use our book knowledge, the stuff we get tested on, as far as it goes. But what are we to do in the realm of our not-knowing? Knowledge is the stuff of an education, but wisdom also requires knowing how little we know. And the stores of our not-knowing are limitless. That sense of the limits of knowledge begins with the physical world—think of dark matter and sticky stuff—and works its way inside. How are we to navigate our emotional lives without charts? There is a quatrain by the Spanish poet Antonio Machado, just four lines of poetry, that speaks to this. Machado writes:

> *People possess four things*
> *that are no good at sea:*
> *anchor, rudder, oars*
> *and the fear of going down.*

I grew up on the Atlantic Ocean, and, like many of you, I know the importance of a set of oars, a rudder, an anchor, and even a healthy fear of the deep to remind us to play it safe. But no, says Machado, "People possess four things / that are no good at sea: / anchor, rudder, oars / and the fear of going down." What's the point? The point is, why go to the same islands all the time? Why have the same thoughts all the time?

Why not abandon oneself to something greater and end up somewhere new, somewhere heretofore unimagined?

I don't have to tell you that the world on your graduation day is faster and more layered than mine was or that of your teachers. The human condition is always complex, but we knew much less about it than you do. The challenges are much more "in your face" than they were for us. It isn't only the events surrounding 9/11, or the latest stomach-churning reports from the Mideast, but the distress in faraway places less in the news, and here at home the needs of our neighbors, and forever and always the continuing effort to make our society freer, safer, and more tolerant. For you, there will be new dangers and new challenges. Remember that Greek fellow, Heracleitus, who said, "We never step into the same river twice"? Talk about understatement!

Oh, and it's a media-happy world that wants to rub our noses in the velocity of change. Given the flood of information, and misinformation, and the speed of our society, if you are to stay in touch with your inner self and hold on to your dreams, you will need a sense of proportion, and of ends and means, and of both reality and possibility.

Today, perhaps more than ever, philosophy and imagination are not luxuries. They are not just personal pleasures or college electives. They are survival skills, and we ignore them at our peril. I urge you to remember that and not to slight your dreams or your inner lives in the rush of jobs and real estate.

All parents want their children to be happy and secure, to make fewer compromises than they had to, to be able to work less and play more, and to validate their youthful idealism. Validating our idealism—that's a big one. After all, everyone has to make a living first. Ben Franklin said that happiness is spending less than you earn. They also say that money doesn't buy happiness. I have an idea I'd like to try out on you, a simple idea. I want to suggest to you that, in the final analysis, you will be judged, by others and, just as crucially, by yourself, by what you do for free. By what you do for others for free.

And by the reach of your compassion.

You know, the penalty for education is self-consciousness. There are times when we long to be as instinctive as the animals. Ignorance is bliss, they say. Yet it's that self-awareness through language, that sometimes nerve-wracking self-consciousness, that is humankind's unique strength. We not only know, we know we know. Therefore, we have the ability to change our minds.

It can be excruciating to play devil's advocate on an issue about which one feels passionately. That's why they call it *devil's* advocate." Yet we like to say that one shouldn't judge another human being until one has walked a mile in his or her moccasins. Do we mean it? I'm not suggesting you overturn your values, but that you be willing to look at the other side of every argument. In an age of fluid borders and weapons of mass destruction, our future depends on people who are able to see both sides. To do so on an inflammable topic, when you and your opponents are in pain, is more than difficult, it is heroic.

And that ability to think for yourself, whether in serenity or turmoil, is the core of a university education.

I'll conclude my remarks with a poem, but first I want to thank President Edmondson and the Alfred trustees for inviting me back to campus, poet and professor Ben Howard for nominating me to speak to you, and emeriti professors Daniel Sass and David O'Hara for putting up with me years ago.

To the Class of 2002, big congratulations. You made it to the finish line. You also made it to the start line. After the long good-bye, the big hello. Look after your insides. Remember to do something for others. Try to be awake. Don't be timid. I believe in dumb luck, but you have to make yourself available. And above all, enjoy yourself. A character in a Kingsley Amis novel says, "There aren't many benefits to sanity, but one of them is being able to tell what's funny."

I'll end by reading a poem called "White Clover." Where I live, the neighborhoods were once farmland. The cows ate clover, and now little white clover blossoms pop up on the lawns.

> *"White Clover"*
> *Once when the moon was out about three-quarters*
> *and the fireflies who are the stars*
> *of backyards*
> *were out about three-quarters*
> *and about three-fourths of all the lights*
> *in the neighborhood*
> *were on because people can be at home,*
> *I took a not so innocent walk*
> *out among the lawns,*
> *navigating by the light of lights,*
> *and there there were many hundreds of moons*
> *on the lawns*
> *where before there was only polite grass.*
> *These were moons on long stems,*
> *their long stems giving their greenness*
> *to the center of each flower*
> *and the light giving its whiteness to the tops*
> *of the petals. I could say*
> *it was light from stars*
> *touched the tops of flowers and no doubt*
> *something heavenly reaches what grows outdoors*

and the heads of men who go hatless,
but I like to think we have a world
right here, and a life
that isn't death. So I don't say it's better
to be right here. I say this is where
many hundreds of core-green moons
gigantic to my eye
rose because men and women had sown green grass,
and flowered to my eye in man-made light,
and to some would be as fire in the body
and to others a light in the mind
over all their property.

Marvin Bell, selected in 2000 as Iowa's first poet laureate, is
the author of sixteen books of poetry and is a teacher at the
University of Iowa Writer's Workshop.

SEAMUS HEANEY

University of North Carolina at Chapel Hill, 1996

Class of '96,

Today's date, May 12, will always be a memorable one for you, and for me, too. From here on, the mark of the tar is upon all of us, academically and indelibly: So let us rejoice in that, because now we fare forth as Tar Heels of the mind, and the world where we are to make our tarry mark in lies all before us.

But then, when it comes to faring forth, today's date, May 12, has always been an auspicious one. Especially in my native province of Ulster, for long ago it was designated a kind of second May Day, the official start of the summer season; and so May the twelfth became the day when the great hiring fairs took place at towns all over the countryside, when working men and working women would assemble there to be hired out for another term to new masters and mistresses. The hiring fair was a cross between a commencement day and a slave market; it was a carnival shadowed by the tyranny of economic necessity, but it did produce a real sense of occasion. It was a hosting of the local clans, and it brought the singer and the musician and the whole community onto the streets, with all their wares and in all their finery; so I thought that I could celebrate this great hosting of the clans here at Chapel Hill and celebrate the old links that have been established between Ulster people who emigrated to North Carolina in the eighteenth century and who played such an important part in the founding of this university—people like the Rev. David Ker, the university's first presiding professor, a graduate of Trinity College, Dublin—I thought I could celebrate that old connection and celebrate, of course, my own new one here today by quoting from a ballad I used to hear when I was growing up in County Derry. It tells the story of a young woman setting out with high hopes of romantic adventure on May the twelfth, to the May Fair at Magherafelt, which is the one sizable town in our part of the country. But it begins like this:

I am a bouncing fair young girl,
my age is scarce sixteen,
and when I'm dressed all in my best
I look like any queen;
bright, young, at play, who wants a way
to go and sell her wares,
on the twelfth of May I made my way
to Magherafelt May Fair.

My mother's caution unto me
was not stay late in town,
for if you do, my father and I
both on you we will frown.
Be wise and shun bad company
and of young men do beware—
how smart you be, don't make too free
in Magherafelt May Fair.

Well, I would like to quote the whole thing, but at this stage it's enough that the bouncing fair young girl has started on her journey; like the heroine of a thousand other ballads, she has roamed out on a May morning to encounter whatever fortune puts in her way. And over the years, because of her confidence and buoyancy, she has become for me the guardian angel of all such moments of faring forth; for it matters very little on occasions like this whether you are the tomboy daughter of God-fearing rural parents in nineteenth-century Ulster or the atheist heir of tobacco barons in our own date—what matters at these occasions is not the economic givens of your background but the state of readiness of your own spirit. In fact, the ability to start out upon your own impulse is fundamental to the gift of keeping going upon your own terms, not to mention the further and more fulfilling gift of getting started all over again—never resting upon the oars of success or in the doldrums of disappointment, but getting renewed and revived by some further transformation.

Getting started, keeping going, getting started again—in art and in life, it seems to me this is the essential rhythm not only of achievement but of survival, the ground of convinced action, the basis of self-esteem and the guarantee of credibility in your lives, credibility to yourselves as well as to others. So this rhythm is what I would like to talk about briefly this morning, because it is something I would want each one of you to experience in the years ahead, and experience not only in your professional life, whatever that may be, but in your emotional and spiritual lives as well—because unless that underground level of the self is preserved as a verified and verifying element in your makeup, you are going to be in danger of settling into whatever profile the world prepares for you and accepting whatever profile the world provides for you. You'll be in danger of molding yourselves in accordance with laws of growth other than those of your own intuitive being.

The world, for example, expects a commencement speaker to arrive with a set of directives, a complete do-it-yourself success kit, which he or she then issues to the graduating class; the commencement speaker's appointed role is to provide a clear-cut map of the future and a key to navigating it as elegantly and profitably as possible. To be a mixture of Polonius and Tiresias, of bore and of bard. But while that is what the world prescribes, the inner laws of this particular speaker's being make him extremely anxious about laying down laws or mapping the future for anybody. In fact, this speaker believes that all those laws and directions have to be personal discoveries rather than prescribed routes; they must be part and parcel of each individual's sense of the world. They are to be improvised rather than copied, they are to be invented rather than imitated, they are to be risked and earned rather than bought into. Indeed, I have to say that for me, this very commencement address has been a matter of risk and improvisation from the moment I said I would do it, because I kept asking myself how I could reconcile my long-standing aversion to the know-all with a desire to say something worthwhile to you.

I therefore did what I increasingly do in moments of crisis nowadays: I asked my daughter what I should do. "Just be yourself, Dad," she said. "Talk about yourself. Tell them a few stories." And this advice was a great relief to me because I thought, "Yes, that's true. Some of the greatest wisdom speakers in the world went about their work that way. So, Seamus, what was good enough for Aesop and for Jesus should be good enough for you. Relax. For a start, for a start, tell them something about getting started."

Like for example, the Russian poet and novelist Boris Pasternak's definition of talent. Talent and the art of writing is "boldness in face of the blank sheet." The sheer exhilaration of those words is already enough to convince you of their truth, the truth that getting started is more than half the battle. One of the great Sufi teachers expressed the same wisdom in a slightly different way. "A great idea," he said, "will come to you three times. If you go with it the first time, it will do nearly all the work for you. Even if you don't move until the second time, it will still do half the work for you. But if you leave it until the third time, you will have to do all the work yourself."

My own story in this regard, however, is more a story about a false start, although it is indeed a story about the importance of getting started from that first base of your being, the place of ultimate suffering and ultimate decisions in each of you, the last ditch and the first launching pad. When I was in primary school, I was once asked to do a composition entitled "A Day at the Seaside"—a common, indeed a predictable subject in a country school in Northern Ireland years ago. So I wrote about the sunlit sand, of the yachts in the bay, of the perfect sand castles and of diving in the pool, even though the weather was usually rainy and it was a coal boat rather than a yacht in the bay and I was a farmer's son who couldn't have passed through the University of Carolina because I couldn't in fact swim at all, never mind diving into a pool. But my chief lyrical effort was reserved for the description of the bucket and the spade I said I had used at the beach. The sky-blue enameled inside of the bucket, as bright as a graduating class at the University of North Carolina, and the technicolor outside, all its little canary yellows and greenfinch greens and canary yellows. And then I also praised the little spade for being so trimly shafted, so youngster-friendly, so small and scaled-down. And so I got my grade for making up a fantasy and delivering the conventional goods, pictures I had seen on postcards of other people's days at the seaside. But years later what came back to me was the thing I did not describe, the truth I had suppressed about a day which had actually been a day of bittersweet disappointment. An account of what had actually happened would have been far more convincing as a piece of writing than the conventional account I had rendered up, far truer to life altogether.

I have to say this, even if is on Mother's Day, but when my mother was out for the day—indeed, especially when she was out for the day—she was a frugal woman, far too self-denying and far too much in thrall to the idea of keeping going to indulge herself or her children in the luxury of catchpennies that she would see like buckets and spades. After all, we were only out for the day; next morning we'd be back on the land, up in the morning for our porridge, out to the field to bring the cows to the byre and after that to deliver the milk to our neighbors. But still, in her mother's heart, she desperately wanted to do something for us, so off she went to a hardware store and bought not the conventional seaside gear that we desired but a consignment of down-to-earth farm equipment which she could utilize when she went home: Instead of bucket and spade, she brought us a plain tin milkcan and a couple of wooden spoons, durable items indeed, useful enough in their own way, but wooden spoons for God's sakes, totally destructive of all glamour and all magic. I hope it will be obvious why I tell you this: I want to avoid preaching at you but I do want to convince you that the true and durable path into and through experience involves being true to the actual givens of your lives. True to your own solitude, true to your own secret knowledge. Because oddly enough, it is that intimate, deeply personal knowledge that links us most vitally and keeps us most reliably connected to one another. Calling a spade a spade may be a bit reductive, but calling a wooden spoon a wooden spoon is the beginning of wisdom. And you will be sure to keep going in life on a far steadier keel and with far more radiant individuality if you navigate by that principle.

Luckily, in a commencement address you only have to get started and keep going. Luckily for you and for me there is no necessity to start again. But for you today, Class of 1996, starting again is what it is actually all about. By graduating from this great and famous university, you have reached a stepping-stone in your life, a place where you can pause for a moment and enjoy the luxury of looking back on the distance covered; but the thing about stepping-stones is that you always need to find another one up there ahead of you. Even if it is panicky in midstream, there is no going back. The next move is always the test. Even if the last move did not succeed, the inner command says move again. Even if the hopes you started out with are dashed, hope has to be maintained. Back in Magherafelt May Fair, for example, our young woman didn't dazzle the crowd as thoroughly as she had hoped she would. The song ends like this:

> *So I bade them all good evening*
> *and there I hoisted sail,*
> *Let the best betide my countryside,*
> *my fortune never fail.*
> *Then night coming on, all hopes being gone,*
> *I think I will try elsewhere,*
> *at a dance or a wake my chance I'll take*
> *and leave Magherafelt May Fair.*

Class of 1996, Tar Heels of the mind, when I said at the beginning that the world was all before you, I was echoing what the English poet John Milton said at the end of his great poem "Paradise Lost." And I am not the first one to have echoed that line. Almost a century and a half after Milton wrote about Adam and Eve being driven out of Eden, into history, having to keep going by the sweat of their brow, Milton's words were echoed by another English poet, William Wordsworth, at the start of his epoch-making autobiographical poem, "The Prelude." By making the entry into adult experience an adventure rather than a penalty, Wordsworth was announcing the theme I have addressed this morning; he was implying that history, and our individual lives within history, constantly involve the same effort at starting again and again.

Whether it be a matter of personal relations within a marriage or political initiatives within a peace process, there is no surefire do-it-yourself kit. There is risk and truth to yourselves and the world before you. But there is a pride and joy also, a pride and joy that is surging through this crowd today, through the emotions of your parents and your mothers particularly on Mother's Day, your families and your assembled friends. And through you yourselves especially. And so, my fellow graduates, make the world before you a better one by going into it with all boldness. You are up to it and you are fit for it; you deserve it and if you make your own best contribution, the world before you will become a bit more deserving of you.

Nobel Prize–winning Irish poet Seamus Heaney is the author of many collections of poetry, three critical volumes, and The Cure at Troy, *a version of Sophocles'* Philoctetes.

ROBERT PINSKY

Dear new fellow alumni, and dear fellow parents: I will talk to you for less than fifteen minutes, as plainly and realistically as I can. I am not going to try to be funny and I will try to avoid baloney. I want to talk to you about graduation from college and American social class.

Toward the end, I will give you three examples of the language or feeling of social class as it applies to our lives. All three examples suggest that we Americans like to avoid the idea of social class, partly for excellent, patriotic reasons and partly because it makes us scared and nervous.

I propose to you that commencement is a good occasion to remember that democracy is not only political, a system of government, it is also a social idea. An idea that makes us nervous, because we are of two minds about it.

What commences at commencement for you graduates is life in a new, elite category. By getting your degree, you join an elite. We use that word with approval, about sports teams, cars, credit cards. "Elite" is good but "elitist" is bad.

We Americans like to reject class as an idea: We don't like to be snobs. But "high class" is good and "low class" is bad and "no class" is even worse. In my New Jersey, "high class" is praise. But as the song says, sometimes it is just a lie.

It is a compliment to call someone a "gentleman," but that

word comes from a set of values where someone who works is not as good as someone who doesn't work: an Old World or Anglophile idea that the gentleman who inherits a rank and property is socially higher than the peasant or artisan whose bread and place in the world depend on being paid for your work and skills.

Feminist reservations about the word "lady" are related to this doubleness about the word "gentleman."

An American ideal reverses the old snobbery. That newer ideal is that it is better and nobler to be rewarded for what you know and what you do than for who your parents were: better to be rewarded for the work you accomplish than for your inherited status.

But before we congratulate ourselves too much, maybe it is appropriate to remind ourselves that we are far from innocent of pursuing status, rank, place in the world. The pursuit of social approval is a significant part—not all, but part—of what the caps and gowns and music and speeches symbolize.

Besides the love of knowledge, and even more maybe than the love of pleasure or gain, we love the admiration of others: approval from our social setting. Will people admire how much I get? Or how much I learn? Or how much good I do?

The part of each graduate that we call "idealistic" has some feeling that the competitions and desires of life may grind away at the idealism.

The part of each graduate that we call "materialistic" has some feeling that material values may wear themselves out.

In dealing with those conflicts, I offer you the notion that at our best moments we Americans manage to make a democratic moral ideal out of what was once a snobby or antidemocratic term—high-class, elite, aristocratic, gentlemanly, noble, the whole dictionary of such terms.

Monty Python has its "Upper Class Twit of the Year" contest; I suppose the corresponding American stereotype would be "Ivy League Jerk of the Year" or "Educated Fool of the Month."

But the idea of being noble, or classy, has its positive, democratic side as well.

Here is the first of my three concrete examples: my father, Milford Pinsky, went to college for one week. It was a junior college. It operated at night, in the building of the high school where he had just graduated. The time was the Great Depression, and he worked during the day.

His first assignment in English Composition was to write an essay on the topic, "What Is a Gentleman." My dad was an athlete, a good-looking boy, and when he turned in his paper, something about him made the teacher accuse him of plagiarism. The teacher made the accusation; it was unjust. My father quit the course; I don't know how much the incident had to do with his never returning to college.

It seems as if the paper was so good the professor couldn't believe it was original, though it was. My father—who died this year—could remember one thing about that composition he wrote. In it, he said something like this: A gentleman considers the well-being of other people more than his own.

That is the aristocratic principle at its best. Maybe the professor thought Milford Pinsky had cribbed it from Henry James, who says something similar in *Portrait of a Lady.*

My second example comes from the writing of W.E.B. DuBois, the great American cultural and political writer. As a scholarly Black man of his time, DuBois had to engage a philosophy that in the wake of the Civil War and Emancipation and the problems facing American Black people seemed a plausible notion: Educate a generation of cooks and carpenters first, then after they grow up, a generation of clerks and tradespeople, and then maybe after that a generation of teachers, and after something like a century, then educate scholars, scientists, doctors, lawyers, scholars, poets, philosophers.

"No!" said DuBois. That idea, though plausible, was corrosive to him. Teach cooks to cook and engineers to engineer and thinkers to think, he says—and teach fools to be dilettantes. My example is the conclusion of his great essay "On the Training of Black Men." Please notice the language of gilded halls, of knights in armor, the graciousness, the elegant blank verse cadences:

I sit with Shakespeare and he winces not. Across the color line I move arm in arm with Balzac and Dumas, where smiling men and welcoming women glide in gilded halls. From out the caves of evening that swing between the strong-limbed earth and the tracery of the stars, I summon Aristotle and Aurelius and what soul I will, and they come all graciously with no scorn nor condescension. So, wed with Truth, I dwell above the Veil. Is this the life you grudge us, O knightly America?

In the great art of the past, in other words, and in its availability to everyone, is a principle at once democratic and noble. Access to the best of the past is a mark of dignity, of being elite. Making that heritage of the best available to all is the opposite of elitist.

As graduates of Rutgers, we can be proud that men and women of color attended and graduated from Rutgers long before Princeton. Paul Robeson grew up in Princeton, New Jersey; Princeton University at the time was very Southern in attitude and population. We can be ashamed that as recently as when I was at Rutgers there were fraternity houses that did not admit Black members—that was no-class, ignoble. But we can be proud that we were were high-class enough to graduate Paul Robeson.

As a land-grant, state institution that is also one of the oldest universities in the country, Rutgers is elite in a special sense. Are we proud of that? Of course. Should we take it as a responsibility to be above automatic pecking orders and shallow ideas of superiority? Of course.

My third and final example is from the New Jersey poet William Carlos Williams, of Rutherford. We may refer proudly to Williams more often than we ponder his poems—too many people know him only for the little ones about the wheelbarrow or the plums.

Williams was devoted to his immigrant grandmother, and in a characteristically American way he was proud of her struggle. My New Jersey is full of immigrant groups that are proud to be here and proud of how they got here and where they came from. We are patriotic about the noble mix of ethnic and cultural elements. The name "patriotism" is often given to aggressively mindless, ugly sentiments. Here is a truly patriotic poem by William Carlos Williams, telling a profoundly democratic, familiar American story, the story about the nobility of struggle, the hard work of a lady he admires, to whom he pays courtly admiration for bringing him into that aristocracy of effort and his ancestral land:

> *"Dedication for a Plot of Ground"*
> *This plot of ground*
> *facing the waters of this inlet*
> *is dedicated to the living presence of*

Emily Dickinson Wellcome
who was born in England; married;
lost her husband and with
her five year old son
sailed for New York in a two-master;
was driven to the Azores;
ran adrift on Fire Island shoal,
met her second husband
in a Brooklyn boarding house,
went with him to Puerto Rico
bore three more children, lost
her second husband, lived hard
for eight years in St. Thomas,
Puerto Rico, San Domingo, followed
the eldest son to New York,
lost her daughter, lost her "baby,"
seized the two boys of
the oldest son by the second marriage
mothered them—they being
motherless—fought for them
against the other grandmother
and the aunts, brought them here
summer after summer, defended
herself here against thieves,
storms, sun, fire,
against flies, against girls
that came smelling about, against
drought, against weeds, storm-tides,
neighbors, weasels that stole her chickens,
against the weakness of her own hands,
against the growing strength of
the boys, against wind, against

the stones, against trespassers,
against rents, against her own mind.

She grubbed this earth with her own hands,
domineered over this grass plot,
blackguarded her oldest son
into buying it, lived here fifteen years,
attained a final loneliness and—

If you can bring nothing to this place
but your carcass, keep out.

We know that story. It is a typical New Jersey hero story: Puerto Rico, the Azores, lost families, rebuilt families, rent, trespassers, working the earth, real estate, family custody battles, a generation raised by the grandmother. It is an American hero story, William Carlos Williams's tale of his noble grandmother, a great lady.

We recognize that kind of story, and we recognize the tone Williams takes in telling it: a tone that is brusque, proud, affectionate, irreverent, and down-to-earth. By telling his grandmother's story in that tone, and in poetry—poetry, an art that is associated with the royal courts of Europe—Williams affirms his democratic, American notion of what is noble, superior, worthy of the gilded halls in DuBois's paragraph, worthy of ladies and gentlemen as defined by Milford Pinsky and by Henry James's Isabel Archer. Williams's grandmother made that family "landed" as in "landed gentry" as well as in "just got off the boat." He is proud of her, and he says if you can't honor her—keep out!

"Keep out!"—that plain. The story Williams tells is real, and above snobbery. One of the most pervasive American snobberies, one we tend to allow ourselves exactly because we are uneasy with the notion of social class, is the snobbery of education: what degrees you have; where you were educated. Please, dear graduates, let's not preen ourselves on having attended a "good school;" we know the point is what we have done at our good school. Please, let's be above overvaluing ranks, titles, degrees. Let's look to what is real.

All degrees are honorary; that is, their meaning and value depends completely on what was really done to earn them.

Imitating Williams's tone as best I can, I say to you graduates: Congratulations on your work, and on your high-born, democratic heritage, and may you bring something to it beside your carcass: If not, keep out.

Robert Pinsky, former Poet Laureate of the United States, is an award-winning poet who teaches at Boston University and is the poetry editor of Slate *magazine.*

PUBLIC FIGURES

We make some changes.
But mostly changes make us.

—*Mason Cooley*

MADELEINE K. ALBRIGHT

Thank you for the introduction. It's a pleasure to be back here at Wellesley, where the memories are good, the welcome is warm, the campus is lovely, and all the students have good posture.

To the Class of 1995, I say congratulations. Today is the payoff for all your long hours of studying, late nights in the library, and exams. Graduation is one of the four great milestones in life. The others are the day you were born, the day you die, and the day you finally pay off your student loan.

In the years ahead, you will look back upon this commencement ceremony and realize that this was the very day and hour you began to forget everything you learned in college. You will find slipping from your mind the carefully memorized names of eighteenth-century composers, European monarchs, and the various body parts of dissected frogs. But as your hopes for hitting a jackpot on *Jeopardy!* fade, you will find that the more profound aspects of a Wellesley education endure.

According to the Wellesley brochure, students develop here a sense of history, a capacity for critical reasoning, an awareness of differing cultures, and a passion for justice.

To the extent this description is accurate—and from your faces, I can see it is true—you will be grateful for the rest of your lives.

In school, grades and test results measure accomplishment. You know what is expected and where you stand. But once you leave school, you will have to rely upon an inner compass, for only you can set the standards by which your life will be measured. Each day, you will face decisions in which your sense of purpose will compete against temptations, distractions, and confusions. You will often be uncertain, for the path to a life of fulfillment and accomplishment is nowhere clearly marked.

The choices and challenges you will face as individuals in the years ahead have their parallel in those now facing our nation.

During the Cold War, the yardsticks of global politics were widely acknowledged; the scoreboard was a map that colored some countries red and others red, white, and blue. Every night on Cronkite or Huntley-Brinkley, we would learn which side had the most troops, the biggest stockpile of strategic weapons, and the most citizens hitting golf balls on the moon.

But the standards of success in the new world are less clear. Here, too, an inner compass is required to select the right goals, establish accountability, and fulfill potential. Here, too, we will find essential the qualities nurtured at Wellesley—a sense of history, a capacity for critical reasoning, an awareness of different cultures, and a passion for justice.

Today, we face not one enemy, but rather many dangers, as well as opportunities that have been a long time coming and that—if squandered—may be a long time coming again.

Just as individuals must overcome temptations and distractions, so our country must overcome internal divisions and a tide of isolationist thinking that is stronger today than at any time since the 1920s.

Legislation now pending in Congress would end UN peacekeeping, pull the plug on support for human rights and democracy overseas, threaten our long-standing commitments to the Middle East, turn our backs on the poor and persecuted around the globe, and undermine our efforts to prevent pollution and counterterrorism and transnational crime.

One leading Republican senator predicts that, if current proposals are approved, America will end up "with as visible and viable an international role as Ghana."

This outcome is not acceptable.

America is a nation with global interests and responsibilities. Some may find that a burden, but for most of us, it is a source of great pride.

The fact is that it matters when America succeeds, as we just have, in gaining global agreement to extend forever the treaty barring new nations from developing nuclear weapons. That is a gift to the future.

It matters when America takes the lead in supporting the peacemakers over the bomb throwers in tinderbox regions such as the Middle East and Northern Ireland.

It matters when America organizes an international coalition to restore democracy to Haiti, end the horrible violations of human rights there, and give the people of that country the chance to build a decent life at home, rather than risk their lives at sea.

It matters when America contributes generously to the first international war crimes tribunals since Nuremberg; because the perpetrators of ethnic cleansing must be held accountable, and those who see rape as just another tactic of war must answer for their crimes.

Finally, it matters that we have an administration that understands that international economic and social progress depends on respect for women and women's rights.

This fall, I will lead the American delegation to the Fourth Global Conference on the Status of Women. We will stress there this truth: When women have the power and the knowledge to make their own choices, birth rates stabilize, environmental awareness increases, the spread of sexually transmitted disease slows, economic opportunity expands, and socially constructive values are more likely to be passed on to the young.

Unfortunately, today, in countries around the world, appalling abuses are being committed against women. These include coerced abortions and sterilizations, children sold into prostitution, ritual mutilations, dowry murders, and official indifference to violence.

Some say that all this is cultural and that there's nothing we can do about it. I say it's criminal and it's the responsibility of each and every one of us to stop it.

Let us be clear: We strive to be aware of ethnic, racial, and religious differences not to find excuses for actions that are wrong, but to ensure the tolerance and understanding upon which freedom and civility depend.

Last year, in Croatia, I visited a farm in what was once a pretty town called Vukovar. There, beneath a pile of rusted refrigerators and scraps of farm equipment, is a shallow grave containing the bodies of two to three hundred human beings. These dead were not the victims of "heat of battle" violence; they were not—in the terminology of the soldier—collateral damage. They were men and women like you and me; boys and girls like those we know; intentionally targeted and massacred not because of what they had done, but for who they were.

During his diplomatic career, my father served as ambassador from what is now the former Czechoslovakia to what is now the former Yugoslavia. He understood the depth of nationalist passions. And he described them as "a permanent, vital and influential force for good and evil."

It was his experience, as it is ours, that national pride can be the custodian of rich cultural legacies; it can unite people in defense of a common good; it can provide a sense of identity and belonging that stretches across territory and time.

But as the current outrages in Bosnia illustrate, when pride in "us" curdles into hatred of "them," the result is a narrowing of vision and a compulsion to violence.

We are all proud of the groups to which we belong. But loyalty to a group cannot excuse the betrayal of universal values.

In respecting the distinctions of physiology, culture, and history that separate us, let us never forget the common humanity that binds us. We are different peoples, but one species—a species distinguished not only by our ability to manipulate our thumbs, but by our ability to think conceptually, create great civilizations, compose masterpieces of art, and ponder the mysteries of life.

Fifty years ago this spring, the American army liberated Buchenwald. They found eighteen hundred naked bodies, stacked like cordwood alongside an incinerator; they watched thousands of those freed die because starvation and disease and abuse had gone on too long; crying themselves, they embraced hollow-eyed children who had forgotten how to cry.

The great lesson of this century is that what happens to people anywhere should matter to people everywhere.

After World War II, the generation that defeated Hitler designed a framework of principle and power that would safeguard freedom, prevent global conflict, extend the rule of law, and expand respect for human rights around the world.

Today, the responsibilities of leadership are in our hands. As

Hillary Rodham Clinton said earlier this year: "There is no comparison to the circumstances in which our parents and grandparents faced the Second World War . . . but neither should there be doubt that we have the same greatness within us."

That is not only a statement of fact. It is a presentation of choice.

A decade or two from now, we will be known as the generation that solidified the global triumph of democratic principles, or as the neoisolationists who allowed totalitarianism and fascism to rise again. We will be known as the generation that laid the groundwork for rising prosperity around the world, or as the neoprotectionists whose lack of vision produced financial chaos. We will be known as the generation that took strong measures to deter aggression, or as the world-class ditherers who stood by while the seeds of renewed global conflict were sown.

Each of us must choose whether to live our lives narrowly, selfishly, and complacently, or to act with courage and faith.

And our nation must choose whether to turn inward and betray the lessons of history, or to seize the opportunity now before us to shape history.

We are not governed by fate or by the alignment of the stars. We are all accountable, for it is the sum of our choices that will determine the kind of America and the kind of world in which we live and our children will live.

It has been said that all work that is worth anything is done in faith. This morning, in these beautiful surroundings, at this celebration of warm memory and high expectation, I summon you in the name of this historic college and of all who have passed through its halls, to embrace the faith that each life enriched by your giving, each friend touched by your affection, each soul inspired by our passion, and each barrier to justice brought down by your determination ennobles your own life, inspires others, and explodes outward the boundaries of what is achievable on this earth.

So congratulations, good luck, and remember always to sit up straight.

Thank you very much.

Madeleine Korbel Albright was the first female US secretary of state. Before her appointment she served as the US permanent representative to the United Nations and as a member of President Clinton's Cabinet and National Security Council.

KOFI ANNAN

Duke University has produced yet another bumper crop of graduates. Congratulations to you all. The first order of business should be a round of applause for the families, faculty, and friends who helped you reach this milestone.

I should also praise the administration for holding this event in a big stadium and not the smaller Cameron arena. It would have been terribly unfair for you to have to camp out in K-ville, as if it were still basketball season, and compete with each other for tickets to your own commencement. After all, you have richly earned your seat here today!

There are few moments in life so powerfully mixed with hope and fear as this one—this day on which you take wing in the wider world; this day on which you and the world start to test each other a bit more seriously.

That world was very different when I graduated more than forty years ago. Even though I went to college here in the United States, as an African my main focus was on my own country, which had just become independent. While we were well aware of the world at large, most of us in Ghana looked inward, and set about running our own country after centuries of colonial rule.

Today, whether you are in Ghana or here in Durham, there

is no such thing as thinking only in terms of your own country. Global forces press in from every conceivable direction.

We are all being influenced by the same tides of change. People, goods, and ideas cross borders and cover vast distances with ever greater frequency, speed, and ease. We are increasingly connected through travel, trade, the Internet, and even sports. The online edition of the *Durham Herald-Sun* can be read in Dublin as if it had been delivered to doorsteps there. And I'm sure there are Blue Devils fans in places you would least expect them!

In such a world, issues that once seemed very far away are very much in your backyard. What happens in South America or Southern Africa—from democratic advances to deforestation to the fight against AIDS—can affect your lives here in North Carolina. And your choices here—what you buy, how you vote—can resound far away. As someone once said about water pollution, we all live downstream.

This interdependence generates a host of new and urgent demands. Towns and villages have their planning boards, fire departments, and recycling centres. Nations have their legislatures and judicial bodies. Our globalizing world also needs institutions and standards.

I am not talking about world government; such an idea never was, and never could be, either practical or desirable. I mean laws and norms that countries negotiate together, and agree to uphold as the "rules of the road." And I mean a forum where sovereign states can come together to share burdens, address common problems, and seize common opportunities.

Global challenges demand global solutions. Our jobs depend not only on local firms and factories, but on faraway markets for the goods they produce. Our safety depends not only on local police forces, but on guarding against the global spread of pollution, disease, illegal drugs, and weapons of mass destruction.

These issues are not new to the United Nations. But for many people, they have been brought into a new and painful focus only recently.

The events of 11 September 2001 showed us all how failed states can end up becoming havens for terrorists, who then visit their destructive acts on others far away. How else to fight such a menace but to come together with cross-border law enforcement and joint efforts to build functioning, democratic societies?

The war in Iraq, and the divisions beforehand over how best to ensure compliance with UN resolutions, have generated apprehension about the implications for our system of collective security, and for the international rule of law. There is deep suspicion and mistrust, both between nations and within them.

Yet people and nations retain the hope of strengthening the foundations of stability, and uniting around common values. The United Nations, for all its imperfections, real and perceived, has built up unique experience. It has brought humanitarian relief to millions in need, and helped people to rebuild their countries from the ruins of armed conflict. It has fought poverty, protected the rights of children, promoted democracy, and raised the profile of environmental issues. We need to build on that experience.

The world is at a critical juncture, and so are you. Job prospects are not as plentiful as you might have preferred. The question typically heard at this time of year—"What are you going to do?"—is a bit more charged than usual.

At the same time, I understand that many of you have used these uncertain times to explore avenues you might not have considered before—such as teaching or other forms of public service in troubled communities in the United States or in some of the world's developing countries. With the ink on your diplomas barely dry, you are coming face-to-face with the unexpected—the turns of events that engage your passions in ways you never could have predicted or thought possible.

I never imagined I would end up where I am. When I joined the United Nations, my plan was to return to Ghana at some point. Instead I was exposed to issues and ideas that drew me ever deeper into the Organization's global mission of peace and development.

The engineers among you might have hopes of working down the road in the Research Triangle, but there might equally be a place for you helping a country emerging from conflict to rebuild its infrastructure.

The lawyers among you might have your eyes on corporate towers in big cities, but there is also some fascinating work to be done helping countries moving toward democracy to write constitutions and build independent judiciaries.

The doctors and nurses among you may be schooled and specialized in all the wonders of modern medicine, but you might also find it rewarding to bring those benefits to people around the world, especially those at risk of dying from preventable illnesses.

The same applies no matter what diploma you are about to receive, from economics to earth sciences. So go ahead and make your plans, pursue your chosen fields, and don't stop learning. But be open to the detours that lead to new discoveries, for therein lies some of the spice and joy of life.

And remember, if this is a world of peril, it is to a far greater degree one of enormous opportunity. And nothing makes a United Nations secretary-general feel more hopeful about the future than seeing you, the Class of 2003, so ready to make your mark on tomorrow. A Duke education is a wonderful gift. Now take it and make it work for all of us. To paraphrase one of Duke's gifted sons, the poet Fred Chappell and now North Carolina's poet laureate: Go and join those who, with palette, loom, and graceful pen, with sculpted stone, and with treatise and debate, build our world and build it up again.

Kofi Annan of Ghana is the seventh secretary-general of the United Nations. He won the Nobel Peace Prize in 2001.

TOM BROKAW

These are moments to be cherished in American life: The realization of a common dream, unique, really, to this land—a college education, a privilege not confined to the well-born or wealthy. Here the working class sits side by side with old and new fortunes. Here new Americans from distant lands and cultures mingle with the sons and daughters of Americans who came on sailing ships, some to proclaim their freedom, others in the holds and chains of slave ships.

I am honored to be with you. I know what is expected of me. Brevity, most of all. Maybe a little humor. Wisdom, or the appearance of it. I am here as a journalist, but I am also here as a husband, a father, and a citizen. That is the four-part harmony of my life, and they are complementary parts; I am incomplete if any one is missing.

I am also a child of the second half of the twentieth century. I was born in 1940, and my earliest memories are of the pain and the glories of World War II; I came of age with the threat of nuclear war in the world—and greatest innocence at home; I stood on the front lines of the battle for civil rights and am haunted still by the personal and political price this nation paid in Vietnam; I can tell you when I first heard Elvis and when I first saw the Beatles. One president was assassinated, another was forced to resign. Communism fell. Women in

America began to take their rightful place. The American family began to take on new forms, alas, too often to the detriment of family members and society.

It was a time of momentous change. Mind-boggling, world-altering, exhilarating, disorienting change. And it was merely an overture for your generation. The sound you hear is a new century, coming fast, with changes and challenges yet unimagined.

This is your time: the twenty-first century. The millennium. It is yours to shape and master. It makes my heart race. I envy you.

You have at your disposal a dazzling assortment of new tools not even imagined not so long ago. The gee-whiz tools of communications and information: cable television, satellites, cell phones, pagers, faxes, and, of course, the king of them all, the personal computer. Who could ask for anything more?

Well, here is a modest suggestion as you lead us into the new century. This will be the cyberspace equivalent of a teenage joyride—reckless and pointless—unless we all apply the lessons of earlier technological revolutions to this one. They almost all have had unexpected consequences, and they are most successful when as much effort and thought is applied to the use of the technology as to the development of it in the first place.

If this new technology becomes simply another means of amusing ourselves, or speeding the transactions of commerce, or communicating simply for the sake of communication, then we will have failed.

If this new technology becomes primarily the province of the privileged, leaving the underclass to wander in cyber wilderness, then we will have failed.

If it becomes merely an instrument of greater invasion into our personal lives, then we will have failed.

This is your technology. Indeed, with the introduction of the cyber age we have fundamentally altered a relationship between generations. This is the first time the kids have taught their parents to drive.

It's where we're headed that concerns me. One of my principal passions is the environment and biological diversity. Cyber technology is a great vehicle for information exchange, mapping, and research. But if we become a nation of shut-ins, more engrossed in a virtual rain forest than the real, thick, seamy, green, vibrant, living, breathing experience, we will be poorer for it.

For all of its capacity, this new technology also is of little use in solving what I believe is the most vexing issue in American life: race. There is no delete button for bigotry. We may be color blind as we surf the Net, but alas, on the street, in the workplace, in our homes and social life, we—more than we care to acknowledge—see life through a prism of pigmentation.

We're doing better. I grew up in apartheid America. Now we have the laws of the land, the richer tapestry of ethnic achievement and prominence, people of courage on all sides of the racial dynamic.

We are increasingly a land of many colors, a geography of Asian, Latino, and African hues against a diminishing backdrop of white European stock.

If we allow racism, expressed either as utter bigotry or dressed up as executive ethnic pride, to metastasize at the current rates, we'll soon find ourselves at an incurable stage, unable to build walls high enough, schools private enough, industries insulated enough to withstand the ravages of racism.

It requires instead that most basic and yet most vexing human condition: an open mind and an open heart. That can be your legacy.

We seem at the moment to be caught in a cycle of easy and cheap distraction. Celebrity has been at once devalued and raised to an artificially high place in our popular culture. Never mind achievement or worth that stands the test of time. A moment in the spotlight of television is life itself for dysfunctional families willing to share their sordid secrets on daytime talk shows; for parents who put their youngsters in the cockpits of small planes on stormy days; for performers who reach ever further into the universe of the outrageous to make an impression; for producers and editors who succumb to the easy temptations of titillation rather than reach for intellectual provocation.

And we encourage that by our benign attention.

Is that how we want to measure, in the closing days of the twentieth century, what has been called the American Century?

We're better than that, or we should be.

I've watched this country go from the vanilla fifties to the psychedelic sixties, to the disco seventies, to the greedy eighties.

Now, in the uncertain nineties, what worries me most is the enduring cynicism in our land about the separation from the traditional institutions of public life, city hall, state house, especially Washington. I cannot remember a time when there was such recognition that the traditional framework of society—of family and faith and community and responsibility and accountability—was in such desperate need of repair.

Your immediate concerns, understandable, are jobs and

careers and relationships. Indeed. They will remain your primary focus for they are about personal happiness and survival.

However, the means by which your time will be measured will be the values that you embrace, the care that you show for each other. Yours can be the age of tolerance and understanding.

To be true to the meaning of this institution and the purpose of its education I urge you to remember the counsel of the late Bartlett Giamatti, Yale president, major league baseball commissioner, and Renaissance man. In a setting quite like this in a lesser-known Eastern institution he said, "You must know that idealism is not a paralyzing but a liberating force and that to strive for principles, even if the journey is never completed, is to tap a vast source of energy, the energy to commit to your best in the brief, precious time that each of us is blessed to have."

Fifty years ago—in 1946—another generation of young Americans marked a special spring in their lives. Together with the British, other Western allies, and especially the Russians, they had just won the war against Hitler and Nazi Germany and imperialist Japan. They had saved the world.

They came home, and they built the America we know today. They kept the peace. They went to college in historic proportions, they married and had families. They built giant industries and small businesses. They gave us great universities and great highway systems. They integrated America. They discovered new cures and gave us new songs. They rebuilt their enemies and stood tall against new adversaries in Moscow and Beijing.

And they didn't whine or whimper.

I am in awe of them.

Fifty years from now let another commencement speaker

stand here and say of your generation: They saved their world, and I am in awe of them.

This is your time. Take it on. Don't be afraid to lean into the wind, love the earth in all of its natural glories, and take care of each other.

We're counting on you.

Veteran reporter Tom Brokaw has been anchor of NBC's Nightly News *since 1983. He is also a best-selling author.*

GEORGE W. BUSH

Yale University, 2001

President Levin, thank you very much. Dean Brodhead, fellows of the Yale Corporation, fellow Yale parents, families, and graduates: It's a special privilege to receive this honorary degree. I was proud thirty-three years ago to receive my first Yale degree. I'm even prouder that in your eyes I've earned this one.

I congratulate my fellow honorees. I'm pleased to share this honor with such a distinguished group. I'm particularly pleased to be here with my friend, the former president of Mexico. *Señor Presidente, usted es un verdadero lider, y un gran amigo.*

I congratulate all the parents who are here. It's a glorious day when your child graduates from college. It's a great day for you; it's a great day for your wallet.

Most important, congratulations to the Class of 2001. To those of you who received honors, awards, and distinctions, I say, well done. And to the C students, I say: You, too, can be president of the United States. A Yale degree is worth a lot, as I often remind Dick Cheney—who studied here, but left a little early. So now we know—if you graduate from Yale, you become president. If you drop out, you get to be vice president.

I appreciate so very much the chance to say a few words on this occasion. I know Yale has a tradition of having no commencement speaker. I also know that you've carved out a single exception. Most people think that to speak at Yale's commencement, you have to be president. But over the years, the specifications have become far more demanding. Now you have to be a Yale graduate, you have to be president, and you have to have lost the Yale vote to Ralph Nader.

This is my first time back here in quite a while. I'm sure that each of you will make your own journey back at least a few times in your life. If you're like me, you won't remember everything you did here. That can be a good thing. But there will be some people, and some moments, you will never forget.

Take, for example, my old classmate Dick Brodhead, the accomplished dean of this great university. I remember him as a young scholar, a bright lad, a hard worker. We both put a lot of time in at the Sterling Library, in the reading room, where they have those big leather couches. We had a mutual understanding—Dick wouldn't read aloud, and I wouldn't snore.

Our course selections were different, as we followed our own path to academic discovery. Dick was an English major, and loved the classics. I loved history and pursued a diversified course of study. I like to think of it as the academic road less traveled.

For example, I took a class that studied Japanese haiku. Haiku, for the uninitiated, is a fifteenth-century form of poetry, each poem having seventeen syllables. Haiku is fully understood only by the Zen masters. As I recall, one of my academic advisers was worried about my selection of such a specialized course. He said I should focus on English. I still hear that quite often. But my critics don't realize I don't make verbal gaffes. I'm speaking in the perfect forms and rhythms of ancient haiku.

I did take English here, and I took a class called the "History and Practice of American Oratory," taught by Rollin G. Osterweis. And, President Levin, I want to give credit where credit is due. I want the entire world to know this: Everything I know about the spoken word, I learned right here at Yale.

As a student, I tried to keep a low profile. It worked. Last year the *New York Times* interviewed John Morton Blum because the record showed I had taken one of his courses. Casting his mind's eye over the parade of young faces down through the years, Professor Blum said, and I quote, "I don't have the foggiest recollection of him."

But I remember Professor Blum. And I still recall his dedication and high standards of learning. In my time there were many great professors at Yale. And there still are. They're the ones who keep Yale going after the commencements, after we have all gone our separate ways. I'm not sure I remembered to thank them the last time I was here, but now that I have a second chance, I thank the professors of Yale University.

That's how I've come to feel about the Yale experience—grateful. I studied hard, I played hard, and I made a lot of lifelong friends. What stays with you from college is the part of your education you hardly ever notice at the time. It's the expectations and examples around you, the ideals you believe in, and the friends you make.

In my time, they spoke of the "Yale man." I was really never sure what that was. But I do think that I'm a better man because of Yale. All universities, at their best, teach that degrees and honors are far from the full measure of life. Nor is that measure taken in wealth or in titles. What matters most are the standards you live by, the consideration you show others, and the way you use the gifts you are given.

Now you leave Yale behind, carrying the written proof of

your success here, at a college older than America. When I left here, I didn't have much in the way of a life plan. I knew some people who thought they did. But it turned out that we were all in for ups and downs, most of them unexpected. Life takes its own turns, makes its own demands, writes its own story. And along the way, we start to realize we are not the author.

We begin to understand that life is ours to live, but not to waste, and that the greatest rewards are found in the commitments we make with our whole hearts—to the people we love and to the causes that earn our sacrifice. I hope that each of you will know these rewards. I hope you will find them in your own way and your own time.

For some, that might mean some time in public service. And if you hear that calling, I hope you answer. Each of you has unique gifts and you were given them for a reason. Use them and share them. Public service is one way—an honorable way—to mark your life with meaning.

Today I visit not only my alma mater, but the city of my birth. My life began just a few blocks from here, but I was raised in West Texas. From there, Yale always seemed a world away, maybe a part of my future. Now it's part of my past, and Yale for me is a source of great pride.

I hope that there will come a time for you to return to Yale to say that, and feel as I do today. And I hope you won't wait as long. Congratulations and God bless.

George W. Bush, the forty-third president of the United States, served as governor of Texas for six years prior to his presidency.

NJABULO S. NDEBELE

Wesleyan University, 2004

President Bennet, honoured guests, graduands, ladies and gentlemen.

I feel so honoured to be here on this special day. I feel even more so for sharing with three other distinguished people the highest honour that an institution of higher learning can confer on an individual. These are occasions that remind us that universities are about relationships of the intellect and its capacity to ennoble, relationships that cut across many conceivable boundaries. That I, a South African who is black, a man, a husband and a father; who has interacted, as a teacher, with many students, teachers, and researchers over the years; and who has from time to time reflected on the human condition through the prism of literary art, have been invited to travel to the United States and to accept an honour of this magnitude from Wesleyan University is an affirmation of a universal value often taken for granted. That Wesleyan University affirms this value regularly is a tribute to those who learn here, who teach here, as well as exercise leadership here.

As I bring you greetings from South Africa, and specifically, from my community of scholars and students of the University of Cape Town, I also want to tell you that this year at our campus we celebrate the one hundred and seventy-fifth year of our history. And you can see how far we have come as South Africa's oldest university.

By a remarkable coincidence, this is the same year in which our country celebrates ten years of democracy. While our country feels new, my university proudly feels somewhat old and hopefully wise and mellow. But we feel so intimidated by the passionate youthfulness of our country that we are doing everything we can to reinvent ourselves, and if we cannot succeed to actually look young, we may at least try to feel so.

I look at more than two hundred years of democracy in the United States and wonder how you feel at this point. Do you feel old and hopefully wise and mellow? Or have you had more than two hundred years of passionate youthfulness? These are not the kind of questions to ask graduating students, who in the glory of their youthfulness, despite being young, are enjoying yet another birth today. Being old is far from their thoughts right now. Yet I'd like to invite you to be old, not in age, but in the ability to stretch the imagination back into history for a brief moment. I'll tell you why.

It's because I'm fascinated by what ten years of one country and more than two hundred years of another country means, about what could possibly connect them.

Ten years ago my country achieved its freedom from tyranny and oppression. But we did not attain our freedom in the usual way. Our road toward liberty could be described as counterintuitive. This means that in a world that had become conditioned to think of conflict, particularly between black people and white people, as something that ends in victors and the vanquished, of the winner taking it all, it was strange, first, not to have had a racial war. And secondly it was strange that the contending races negotiated themselves out of conflict in favor of an outcome with two victors and no losers. Very strange! What kind of people give up power? And what kind of people give up the possibility of attaining it?

What most of us recognized in South Africa, at the very last moment, was just how much we needed one another. We realized that violent confrontation promised only destruction and a long life of shared misery. It was a choice we made. It was a choice against habit, the habit to seek to march into final battle. But there is something deeper about the choice of abandoning habit. It is something we have not reflected on fully in my country.

South Africans have been reflecting on the impact of the past ten years on their lives. Rightly so, they have pointed to achievements that were beyond our imaginations. Within ten years, millions of people have their own houses, clean water, electricity, telephones, and universal early schooling. Major institutions of democracy such as parliament, the constitutional court, and other courts of law are used to resolve disagreement and conflict.

While these achievements are real and substantial, the deeper revolution in South Africa is not sufficiently appreciated. It is that we have not explored fully the implications of counterintuitive solution.

I like to think of this matter this way: Consider the white leaders who had been telling their followers by word and deed, and through the way they organized society into contrasts of black and white, power and powerlessness, wealth and poverty, division and wealth, that they had a divine right to be superior to other people, only for these leaders to declare almost overnight that this view was wrong all along. How do you turn around in this way and retain credibility?

Such leaders faced the fear of loss of credibility, the fear of being thought of as having betrayed their people, of being thought of as having cowardly lost their nerve, and of having become weak at a crucial moment.

Many whites did feel betrayed. Many experienced confusion and tremendous anguish, overnight. We remember one who, in a fit of anger and frustration, took his gun and shot at any black person he came across, killing many. Remarkably many others of his kind recoiled in horror before what they suddenly recognized in themselves.

On the other hand, consider the black leaders, symbolized by Nelson Mandela, who told their followers over decades of struggle that the white man understood only one thing: the language of violence. Freedom would come only at the barrel of a gun. Then one afternoon, on the very day that Nelson Mandela was released and tens of thousands of people waited for him to announce the beginning of a war, he told them instead about responsibility, reminding them about higher goals of freedom. It set conditions for negotiating with the enemy. How do you turn around in this way and retain credibility?

What these events dramatized in an intriguing way was how two camps recognized mutual vulnerability through exposing themselves to considerable risk. In doing so, both sides resisted the attractive habit to be tough. Being tough would have meant going to war at whatever the price. Each would have convinced themselves truth was on their side. But thankfully, our leaders realized that being tough in this kind of way had caused much misery in human history. Caught in the clutches of danger, they discovered a new meaning of toughness as something much harder to do. They discovered that being "tough" was not so much about going to war, but about choosing to avoid it.

I believe there have been remarkable benefits from this that were profoundly human. South Africans gave up one-dimensional ways of thinking about one another. They gave up bias, stereotype, and preconception. In giving up histori-cally determined certitudes about themselves and one another, they sought to become far more tolerant, more open-minded, more accepting of personal or group faults. And that, for me, has been the greatest South African revolution: the transformation of deeply held personal and group attitudes and beliefs.

Perhaps to get a sense of just how far we have come, let us recall what it was like living in South Africa just before we gave up war and violence as a solution to our problems. We remember how arrogant and self-righteous white society and the apartheid government were in those days, and how those attributes of behaviour made them blind to their cruelty and the extent of it. They projected invincibility, as if things would be the way they wanted them to be to the end of time. The South African sun, they said, would never set. Being the most powerful military machine in South Africa, they had terror-ized the entire subcontinent to submission. Their military capability had far outstripped their capacity to make it accountable to a higher moral order. The value of their human-ity and their identity as a people became inseparable from, and even reducible to, their weapons of war. They had become a manipulative state, obsessed with the mechanisms of its own survival.

They had this sense that they could stand up to the whole world, defy global opinion, and do whatever they liked in the pursuit and promotion of their self-interest. In this they sub-jected their own citizens to the kind of constant brutality they meted out to others. In dealing with those they regarded as of lesser human quality than themselves, they were accountable to no higher morality. I remember that far from earning my respect, I deeply feared them. But it was a fear that went with much loathing.

It all seems like a bad dream now. Within a short space of time, the false sense of invincibility gave way to a deeply liberating sense of vulnerability and even humility. That was one of the defining moments of our transformation: this embracing of uncertainty and vulnerability, which at the same time went with the certitude that the past was unsustainable.

I have reflected much on this. What seems to happen in this situation is that at the point at which you recognize mutual vulnerability between yourself and an adversary that won't go away, you signal a preparedness to recognize that there might be new grounds for a common humanity whose promise lies in the real possibility that you may have to give up something of what has defined your reality, handed down from a past that cannot entirely meet your best interests now and in the future. It is the humility that arises when you give up certitudes around what was previously the uncontested terrain of your value system and unsustainable positions derived from it.

It is a delicate psychology that is at play here. Its full potential is possible only through a newly discovered foundation of trust. It is about how to reconstitute identity, meaning, and credibility during that fragile moment when you and your adversary are both in danger of losing them all. It is about recognizing that both of you are caught in a situation of profound need for each other. But it is never easy to reach such a position, and if it can be so difficult for individuals, consider how difficult it must be for entire nations. Few are the moments in history when nations were in a position to accept that they could be wrong, that a value system that stood them so well through centuries may no longer be sustainable. In this, nations would rather go to war and be humiliated by unintended outcomes that showed them just how much they ignored an inner voice of caution, or the pride that forced them to ignore it.

These reflections arise from my challenge to our graduation class to stretch their imagination back into history to try to find what could possibly connect a ten-year democracy with one that is more than two hundred years old. Well, what is this connection?

We still recall with excitement in South Africa the pains, traumas, and finally the pleasures of giving up a past. I believe that for you in the United States, the connection is your capacity to recall how exciting it was to do so more than two hundred years ago. Where do you sense yourself to be at this juncture in this world that all of us live in? Is there reason to contemplate another birth? Is there need for some great leap to be taken? One of the greatest fears of political leadership is the fear of losing it. The question is, has the fear become so inordinate that it has become a real threat to the future?

So much has happened to you since 9/11, when the world was truly in solidarity with you. I wrote to my friends all over the United States, telling them how much I suffered with them. Since then, I experience the world with increasing fear. I see the world becoming more and more divided. I sense that the situation we are in from a global perspective is not fundamentally different from where my country was ten years ago. I sense that the world needs a leading nation, or group of nations, that can reassure, inspire hope, and offer fresh perspectives and new directions. I ask myself what nation or nations could possibly do that. I do not have an unambiguous answer. One moment I know it, the next moment I don't. Of one thing I am certain, though: The evolution of global awareness has led us to yearn for a world that needs to value highly multiple visions of itself. We need leadership to get us there. Where will it come from?

One thing is certain also: War and conquests in the twenty-first century suddenly look distressingly primitive as instruments for conducting the affairs of the world, no matter how advanced the weapons of war. We need a new value system for resolving world conflicts. In that value system the mechanisms for the resolution of conflicts and disputes would be founded on the principle that it is possible and even desirable to achieve mutually affirming solutions, to have mutually respectful victors and no losers. The value system based on the single, predetermined solution, often one that is imposed by force of arms, will not result in mutually affirming outcomes, but can generate powerful human emotions that lead to perpetual global dissonance, anxiety, fear, and despair.

Now, I do have faith in the power of humanity to reinvent itself. In this, every graduation offers that possibility. That is why I am so happy for you, Class of 2004, who are moving out into the world, confident that you will contribute to societal renewal through your infectious enthusiasm and zest for life.

Mr. President, thank you and your great university for honoring me so much, and for giving me the opportunity to share some thoughts that have preoccupied me. May Wesleyan University continue to bring out young people who can think about their world in a new way. I hope that my country and yours can play a vital role in facing the challenge to renew a world which sends out many messages to us about just how much we need one another. We can no longer afford to be blind in continuing to ignore these messages.

Njabulo S. Ndebele is a distinguished poet, activist, and vice chancellor of the University of Cape Town in South Africa.

COKIE ROBERTS

It's very nice to be here. It seems so familiar; I froze the whole time I was here. Here I am again. It's also nice to be in a familiar place because Washington is getting less familiar with every passing day. It's getting harder and harder to explain what's going on there, and we're losing some of our most familiar characters who we used to be able to count on to have continuity.

When I'm in the Boston area, I can't help but think about Tip O'Neill, who, of course, was "Mr. Speaker" for so long, and a great and dear friend. I saw him about a week before he died, and he was at an event to raise money for a scholarship for a student, and he got up and told a story that I just love because he prefaced it by saying Mrs. O'Neill didn't like for him to tell this story. And I thought, Dear Lord, what could it possibly be? The idea of Tip O'Neill telling a risqué story was too tantalizing for words. It started, as so many do, with a man dying, going to heaven, getting to the gates. Saint Peter says, "My son, you have been a good and noble servant of the Lord. You may have any wish you want. What would you like it to be?" And he says, "I want to see the Blessed Mother; I have a question to ask her." Saint Peter says, "Done." So the guy goes in and he meets Mary and she says, "I understand you have a question, my son." And he said, "Yes. You know, over all those centuries, in all that art—every stained-glass window, every statue, every painting—when you're holding the baby Jesus, you look sad. Why is that?" She says, "I wanted a girl."

I must say, it has not always been so familiar at Wellesley. My mother's words, that Diana read, were not her first words about Wellesley, I want you to know. When I came here, as a freshman, it was pouring. I'm the youngest child, and my mother and father, for reasons that still escape me, lo these many years later, decided to drive me to college; this was very unlike them. And we got here and were doing all the usual things, you know, opening the bank account, mama was sewing in name tags and all that stuff. And then, as they drove off and left me behind, drove off the campus in the pouring rain, my mother burst into tears, and said to my father, "We've left our baby in a Yankee, Protestant, Republican school." Every time we tease mom about it, she says, "Well, it's true."

I must say that even though it's cold, I'm glad to have a sunny graduation. It poured on my graduation here too, and we were indoors, and our graduation speaker (this was the year 1964) was McGeorge Bundy. Now, I know that you all weren't born and all that, but he became rather famous and was someone that the Vietnam War was somewhat blamed on. And I think back on that peaceful graduation day, and how nobody thought about such a thing as protest or anything like that. If the poor man had shown up on campus a few years later, he probably would have been stoned.

But it was a different time, and I was thinking about some of the things that made it a different time. And of course one of the things, one of the facts for us as young women, was that the thought of war was not something that really had touched us—and we couldn't imagine it touching us. As the immediate years after that went by, it touched us vicariously through the men that we were involved with. Some of us have children as a result of that war, and we like them, we're very glad that they're there—but it did happen. But the idea that we might be involved was something that never occurred to us, and really has never occurred to women until now. And the first time I was really struck by it was in listening to the congressional debate on the Persian Gulf War.

It was a wonderful and studious debate. It was really Congress at its best—one of those times when it's easy to explain, as opposed to the usual—and I was struck by the language, because people in the House and Senate kept talking about "our men and women in uniform, our men and women in Saudi Arabia, our men and women in the Gulf," and it was just remarkable. We had never heard that before, ever. I mean the dirty little secret is that women have been in our military since the Revolutionary War, but we've never talked about it openly before. And then it struck me that we really had never talked about "our men" either, it had always been "our boys"— "our boys in Vietnam, our boys in Korea, our boys in Europe," which led me to the quite wonderful observation that this was not the first time that a woman had turned a boy . . . into a man.

I am honored to be here, to be back, not only because it's a place I really care about enormously, but because you've had such a fabulous group of graduation speakers in recent years. I mean it's been sort of First Lady Central. I loved the year that you had Barbara Bush, and then she had the sense to bring along Raisa Gorbachev, who, of course, was noted for her philosophy degree. I mean that was it, right? And then Hillary Clinton, of course, recently, before she was First Lady. When I was here the only First Lady that was ever around was

Mei-ling Soong, and that was sort of an interesting situation, but I won't dwell on that.

I did ask Mrs. Clinton about Wellesley, what she thought. I saw her not too long ago, and she said, "Well, things really haven't changed there a lot." She said, "They changed in the middle, but they're back again." And I took that to be an endorsement. I was shocked, though, by something she said a week ago today, about another First Lady, about Jacqueline Kennedy Onassis. And here's what Mrs. Clinton said, quote: "The choices one makes have to be her own." I thought about that, and of course that's true: You do make all kinds of choices and they do have to be your own. But life presents a lot of choices that you don't expect as well. Jackie Kennedy didn't expect to be a widow at age thirty-four. She then had to make choices about how she was going to live that life.

Today would have been my sister's fifty-fifth birthday. She loved the color purple. She would have loved to see the balloons around. She didn't choose to die at fifty-one of cancer, and I didn't choose to have an old age without her. But life presents you with choices that you then have to deal with and adapt to. My mother did not expect my father's plane to fall out of the sky, but at age fifty-eight made the choice to run for office herself, as a widow. So I think there are a lot of choices that are made for you, but there are then things that you do to choose to deal with them in various ways.

I noticed in a letter that I got, as a member of the community, from Diana concerning one of your many controversies. She said, "In an increasingly interdependent and multicultural world, we must find better ways to discover and rally round the common bonds that unite us amid our diversity. At Wellesley, we will continue to provide a learning experience

that prepares women for the complexity of a changing world"—
choices that are thrust on you.

I got my class reunion book yesterday, the 1964 book.
Thank God for it, because I was not prepared for this speech;
I was having to cram. I had thought that I would have plenty
of time, and then I was sent off to do a story about the
Citadel, about a young woman wanting to get into the
Citadel. I tried to keep an open mind, thinking that as I talked
to these young men, "Now, pretend they're women, pretend
they're women, and put everything they say in that context."
But that became really hard because they said things to me
like, "Well, we can't have girls around here, I mean, you
know, what would happen when we get together in the morning and we all pull each other's pants down and stuff?" I
swear to you, they said that. Whew! But it did throw me off
my stride about having a chance to write a speech to you, and
I got home and found that I had my class reunion book, and
I was just struck by the choices that people at our age, thirty
years out of here, feel that they are continuing to make and
having to make, that it is all still sort of in front of them in a
variety of ways.

Let me read you just a few selections here. This one is from
a lawyer who is the mother of a ten-year-old—now that's a
choice that's less open to us than it is to men, to have children
at age fifty. She says:

> On October 1, my employer from the last fourteen
> years ceased to be an independent public company, and
> became a wholly owned subsidiary of another company,
> one that Jay [student commencement speaker at
> Wellesley today] wants to be editor-in-chief of, actually.
> The year leading up to this event was very exciting and

134

busy for me as the company's sole inside lawyer; however, what this change will mean for me in terms of future professional challenge is still not entirely clear. So I'm beginning to think about what I will do when I grow up.

Here's another. This is a college professor. She has grown children, second marriage.

I'm somewhat unnerved by my present stage of life. I'm uncertain about my direction in my work and unsettled by the necessary changes in our family relationships as our kids become independent and we become ever more clearly the older generation. Still, even as I mull over my next steps, I count my many blessings, including a loving family, a happy marriage, and many, many pleasures. I've developed enough sense over the years to know that uncomfortable transitions are necessary for growth to happen. At fifty-one, I guess I'm having growing pains again.

And then this one (this is another lawyer—this might say more about lawyers than life, I'm not sure):

My world is one of transition, both in attitude and in actuality. I feel as though I'm in the middle of one of those books, in which you can choose a number of possible twists to the plot and don't know the end until you get there. I'm still picking plots. I'm not sure I'll know the story line anytime soon. Anyway, I plug along as a lawyer, continue to be fascinated with the development of women's issues, appreciate my friends and supporters more and more, and revel in the warmth of my wonderful family.

I think that this book is actually a fascinating book. It has stories for everyone. I mean Sally Jessy and Oprah could have a wonderful time with it. It does have the whole spectrum of American stories . . . and it is so interesting to me because we were not a very diverse group, and yet we have led somewhat diverse lives. A lot of people ask in the book, "Where is the wisdom of middle age?" A lot of them answer that question very profoundly. It's very clear that their lives have been touched, not only by the tragedies of normal life, the deaths of family members, the loss of people who were close to them, and by the blessings of normal life. But they've also been touched by the particular tragedies of these times that we live in. You tend to think that only you are affected by these things, but let me read from another classmate.

I've been touched by AIDS. A fellow piano teacher spent two awful years trying to stay upbeat in the face of his approaching death. He and his faith were an inspiration to me, but it seemed like such a waste for him to die. I've also been touched by unprovoked violence: A good friend's husband was killed in the massacre at Luby's cafeteria in Killeen, Texas. She's now living on the edge financially. Another professional friend's oldest child, thirty-nine years old with two children, eleven and seven, was killed last week in San Antonio by a couple of teenagers who ambushed him. My friend's willingness to forgive the murderers of her son is also an inspiration to me. She's taking great comfort that his organs have improved the lives of over three hundred other people. Wouldn't it have been better if that good man could have lived out his full life? What can be done about the lack of care of our children, for the lives of others?

And finally, another classmate, touched by the particular times in which we live.

My husband, Ezio, was assassinated in March 1985 by the Red Brigades, and two years later I was asked to enter politics. Why did I enter politics? At the time I was asked to run, I felt that what had been my life up to the moment of Estio's assassination had been destroyed, not by private rage and violence, but by a political act, and that the offer of the candidacy had placed me up against the choice of either trying to put my life back together on the level that I had lived it before the assassination or of becoming an actor in the sphere from which the destruction had come. I felt that the only choice I had was to try to combat destruction as best I could on that level. Another factor which decided me in favor of the candidacy was the fact that I ran on a feminist ticket, and I thought and think that we need more women in politics.

Yes, Jay, yes indeed. We need more women in politics. You talked about Roslyn. The person I like to quote is an assembly-woman in Connecticut who is a plumber by trade, who said when she was talking about the importance of getting involved in public service, "I figured I either had to stop complaining or run for office, and I knew I couldn't stop complaining." It's important of course to have women in politics for all of the reasons that you know about. It is something that I see constantly, the issues that they bring to the fore. But one of them—and this is the place where I think in the end you will have no choice—one of them is that they bring their role as caretakers to the world of politics.

And that is what I see as a theme running through my class book: that you will make that choice no matter what other choice you make, that you will be the caretakers in this society. It's what we do. That's what women do. We're the nurturers, we're the carriers of the culture. And whether you run for president or run the Patriot's Day race or become editor-in-chief of the *New York Times* (though you might want to talk to me before you do that), whether you do, as Hillary said, "make policy or bake cookies" (it's been my experience that one generally does both), that what you will still be doing, no matter whatever else you do, will be being the caretakers.

Ronald Reagan offended people when he said that women should be honored as civilizers. That statement was offensive because he said it to a group of professional women and defined them in terms of their relationship to men. He said they were civilizers of men. But he was right. We are. (I must say that men sometimes make it a little difficult, but that is what we do.) We can't avoid it. And, as I say, in politics, it is the women who are constantly bringing the civilizing issues to the forefront, the caretaking issues, the issues of concern to families and children.

Right now the focus in Congress, on the part of women, is on women's health and all of the myriad issues affecting women's health, from reproductive health, birth control, mammograms, all the way through breast cancer research, all of the things. That is a primary concern to the women in Congress because if they don't do it, nobody else will. I had an experience a few years back where, what the women in Congress do is, you know, they sort of bring women's issues up like Chinese water torture and constantly drip them on the heads of their male companions until finally they get passed. A few years back there was this tremendous effort to get mammograms covered by Medicare, and it was getting very hard to do, and there were not enough women on the appropriate committees to have it in place every step of the way of the process, so one woman who was a lobbyist went to a male friend on a committee and said, "I need you to bring up this mammogram legislation." And he said, "Oh, I can't do that. I did the last bit of legislation for women in the subcommittee. Everybody will think I'm soft on women." And she said, "Nah, just tell 'em you're a breast man." He did. It worked!

But I have to tell you I don't just see this role of women as caretakers in the world that I cover, I see it in the world I live in. Slowly, slowly, slowly but definitely, the workplace is becoming a more humane place because of the presence of women. The idea that time can be taken for family, whether it's having children or caring for sick people or elderly people in your family. That is becoming more possible for the men in the workplace as well as for the women in the workplace because of the fights that we have fought over the last several decades.

But I also do see it in my personal life. Four years ago this time when my sister was dying, she was completely surrounded by a network of caretaking women—her mother, her sister, the nuns who had taught us, the nurses, women doctors, her hairdresser who would come and make her beautiful, and then circles of women around that. My daughter was in college at the time in Princeton. She was taking care of my sister; the women in her class were taking care of her. The women in my profession were saying that somebody would always be there for me—these are busy, journalistic women. The women in Congress were doing the same thing for my mother, supporting her and caretaking her because that was what they understood they needed to do for each other and for her—was to say "Yes" under those circumstances.

What I would say is that it is impossible to shake the caretaker role even if you wanted to, and I will revert just briefly once again to my class book to one hysterical line from a friend saying, "George's parents are still in good health and maintain active lives. We think it's remarkable that his eighty-one-year-old father and seventy-eight-year-old mother look after George's hundred-year-old grandmother, who still lives alone in her Wisconsin farmhouse. May we all do as well." So you can't shake it, but I don't know why you would want to.

Life is long. You have many opportunities ahead of you. You have so many more opportunities than so many people. You are privileged and blessed. And you will have the opportunity to say "Yes" to many different things, but you also will have the opportunity in the saying of "Yes" to say "No" sometimes, to say, "No, it's not right for me, and my family, right now, to take this great job offer." And you know what? Another one will come along. I'm living proof of that. You can do it all. There are times when you have to not do it all at once. There are times when you don't sleep. But you can do it if you have some sense about saying, "This is what's right now, this is where I am now, and this is the care I need to take right now." I think that it is important to look at the long view as you go out of here and realize that there's a long time ahead, and there is time to see it all, to do it all, and to do it in ways that make you proud and happy in the end.

One last reading from a friend:

I've been thinking lately about the changing size of my world, interior and exterior. Our generation grew up with rosy expectations about the economy, about the invincibility of our country, about the boundless possibilities for our lives. Yes, there were much more limited opportunities for women, and nearly unfathomable dangers, such as the threat of nuclear annihilation. But I think most of us felt a personal optimism which our children do not. What they see is a shrinking job market, AIDS, drugs, crime, homelessness, thinning ozone, and more and more cynicism about the possibility of fundamental change. We came of age in a time of hope, of Camelot, when anything seemed possible—and they're growing up in post-Watergate, post-Vietnam, post-decade of greed, crisis of faith.

Now, as many corporate giants downsize, I find myself doing the same. The medium-sized theater company I worked for in the eighties failed, and I'm now working for a smaller one. With one child gone and one back only temporarily from college, my live-in family has shrunk. As my husband considers retirement, we face a smaller income. As hormone changes take their toll, I find myself with less energy. Through my fifty-year-old eyes, even the print has grown smaller.

One of my happiest moments came, though, when I finally discovered, late in my forties, that I didn't have to accomplish something huge in order to succeed. Corollaries of this discovery were that I didn't have to save the world, publish the great American novel, or be Superwoman all the time; however, I could launch a scholarship fund for a deceased Wellesley friend, become a pretty good theater marketing director, and learn to be a more compassionate family member and friend.

The long view: When we were living in Greece, we used to go to this beach at Marathon—just think of it . . . And there was a little museum there, a little tiny museum from well before the Battle of Marathon that you've studied, with artifacts from seven thousand years ago. And you looked in these cases, and there were buttons, there were frying pans, there were mirrors, there was jewelry—and it was remarkable to look at. You could open them and put on—you could put it on and use it right away! It was totally recognizable to the lives of women today. For men, what was in those cases? Well, there were some bows and arrows, and there were some articles of worship, so if you were a soldier or a priest there was something. But if you just went about leading your daily lives, there wasn't something terribly recognizable for you. That's what we have: We have this wonderful, wonderful continuum.

So I say to you, young women of Wellesley, open up those cases. Take up the tools and put on the jewels—of your foremothers and sisters. Go out into this world and take good care of it. Thank you.

Cokie Roberts is a political commentator and best-selling author who has won two Emmys during her thirty-year career in broadcasting.

MARY ROBINSON

Emory University, 2004

Finding a Moral Compass

A s I look out at all of you, I'm instantly taken back to my own graduation as part of the Harvard Law School Class of 1968. Two memories about that day stay with me most. I remember how proud my father was, and as we processed in this morning and I saw parents lining up to take photographs and record the occasion, I saw the same pride and love reflected on their faces today.

I also remember that my father was very indignant about one problem—it was raining that day in Cambridge, Mass. He had come all the way from the west of Ireland, and he did not appreciate that the sun was not shining. That's not a problem, I understand, either today or apparently ever at Emory. I'm told that every time you have this wonderful commencement ceremony, the sun shines. I can only conclude that Emory has influence where it really matters.

The second thought that comes back to me—I remember how uncertain I was about where exactly life would lead me next. I know many of you are feeling that way today. After all, the moment between completing one chapter in life and beginning the next generally produces a mixture of reflection, relief, and regret.

In reflecting now, nearly forty years later, on my own feelings of uncertainty then, I can see that it was also due in part to the uncertainties and turmoil of those times. They were days of great questioning, not only in my native Ireland but also here in the United States. They were times marked by questioning about the Vietnam War and by the struggles in this country for civil rights.

You too have gone through your years of higher education during uncertain times. The terrible attacks of September 11, 2001, here in the United States and their aftermath have left people in this country and around the world feeling less secure, less able to say with conviction that the world is becoming more peaceful, less confident that the future will be better than the past.

As your commencement speaker it is my privilege, and indeed my burden, to offer some words of guidance on how best to steer your way through the uncertainties of today and those that will surely come throughout the rest of your lives.

You might wish that I could offer a simple road map for life or a set of tried-and-true rules that will show you the way. But the reality is that each one of you will need to rely on your own moral compass to find your paths. When you look back many years from now, I believe you'll realize how formative the experience of being here at Emory was during these times in developing your own inner sense of direction, your own sense of obligation to yourself, to your families and communities, and to the world around you—or, rather, two worlds—two very different and divided worlds around you.

You've been able to experience the unfolding of a new century with all its opportunities and challenges within an environment where the pursuit of knowledge was the ultimate aim. Thanks to the guidance of your professors and to the exchange of views and experiences with your fellow students, you've been able to dig deeper and hopefully bring forth richer insights into the probing issues of our day.

You've been given a great gift—one which several thousand million people on this planet will never receive. You've been given time and a space to examine your beliefs and to see the world in all its complexity, not just through your eyes but also through the eyes of others. You've had the opportunity to develop that moral compass, which can guide you though life and help you to stick to your principles.

Professor Martha Nussbaum of the University of Chicago talks about this vital role of the university in her book, *Cultivating Humanity*. She argues that a fundamental responsibility of the university is to ensure that every student is exposed to the basic skills needed for citizenship.

First, an education that inculcates, and I quote, "the capacity for critical examination of oneself and one's traditions—for living what, following Socrates, we may call the examined life."

Second, a curriculum that provides students with a greater knowledge of non-Western cultures, of minorities within their own, of differences of gender and sexuality. And third, the cultivation of narrative imagination or the ability to think what it might be like to be in the shoes of a person different from oneself, to be an intelligent reader of that person's story.

It's worth taking some time today, even as you rightly celebrate your achievements and look forward to new challenges ahead, to consider the extent to which you are now equipped with those skills of citizenship and that moral compass, and what role they will play in your futures.

For me, the compass pointed to a career in the law and public service. I saw this as the best way to try and make a difference and address the issues I felt so deeply about. So I became a lawyer taking cases before the Irish and European courts. I was fortunate to have been involved in cases that affected the reality of people's lives.

For example, legal actions which led to the removal of discrimination against children born out of wedlock, and the achievement of equal pay and opportunity for women in the workplace.

I saw for myself how the law—something written in a book and decided in a courtroom—can sooner or later reverberate back into the lives of people, opening up possibilities and impacting individual circumstances.

Years later, as president of Ireland and then as United Nations high commissioner for human rights, I made it a priority to go to areas of conflict and serve as a witness to the suffering of the victims in places as far apart as Northern Ireland, Rwanda, Chechnya, Colombia, East Timor, Sierra Leone, the Democratic Republic of Congo, and Afghanistan. I witnessed the common yearnings of humanity and the common obstacles that kept some societies from realizing rights for all people.

And by being there and listening—very simply, listening, and showing an ability to take on board the extent of suffering and the fight back—I hoped to help those victims have their voices heard.

In each place I visited, I met women and men who wanted essentially the same things: Fundamental rights to be free from fear and free from want. I found parents just like yours who wanted their children to be healthy and happy and to have an education that would help them get a good start in their lives.

But in each of these conflict zones I also found at times an unwillingness on both sides of the divide to see the "other" or the enemy as an individual with hopes and dreams and with equal rights. I saw how patterns of discrimination in a society drove wedges between communities. And all too often I saw how corrupt and undemocratic governments fueled intolerance and denied people basic rights, thereby precipitating dissent and rebellion.

One of my final responsibilities during my five years as high commissioner was to work with United Nations member-states' governments to achieve a successful outcome of an international conference which sought to address exactly these issues—a conference against racism and intolerance, which took place in September 2001 just days before the horror of 9/11.

Tragically, even a conference intended to uphold and defend the inherent dignity of every person was used by some to further hatred and spread messages of intolerance and racism. Some members of the Emory community have argued that I didn't do enough in my role as high commissioner to prevent or speak out against the deplorable anti-Semitism which surfaced both in the negotiations between governments before the conference and in the wider deliberations during the conference itself.

Others were unhappy with the human rights analysis I made of the terrible ongoing conflict in the Middle East. Let me just say again that I find the very concept of anti-Semitism repulsive, that I have taken action against it all my life, that my only motivation at all times has been to further the cause of human rights for all people.

I think we must all reflect that there is still hurt and pain, which the Durban process evoked. I decided to mention this situation directly today for two reasons. First, because I believe strongly, as President [Jim] Wagner has stressed, that all of us have a responsibility to hold fast to the ideals on which higher education rests—truth, justice, and reasoned dialogue.

As you've heard, I recently was honored by an invitation from Professor Harold Berman, who in fact was a teacher of mine at the law school in Harvard, to join with President Jimmy Carter as an adviser of the World Law Institute here at Emory University, which would provide further opportunities for just such a reasoned dialogue.

And the second reason I mentioned these events is because I hope it will help you remember that at each step in your lives you'll be required to make judgments, to assess a situation, to form a view, often in less-than-ideal circumstances. There rarely, if ever, will be a perfect result. The test will be whether you are able to keep on and stay true to your own moral compass by listening acutely to the views of others around you.

My fellow countryman Seamus Heaney, who addressed you last year, the Nobel Prize laureate in literature whose collected papers will enrich the wonderful program in Irish literature that President Wagner described, said it better than I ever could at a similar occasion, though not last year.

He said, and I quote, "By graduating from this great and famous university, you have reached a stepping-stone in your life, a place where you can pause for a moment and enjoy the luxury of looking back on the distance covered, but the thing about stepping-stones is that you always need to find another one up there ahead of you. Even if it is panicky in midstream, there is no going back. The next move is always the test. Even if the last move did not succeed, the inner command says move again. Even if the hopes you started out with are dashed, hope has to be maintained."

So my simple wish for you today and in the future is that the next stepping-stone will always be in your sight. Warmest congratulations to you all, and I am delighted to join you as part of the Class of 2004. Thank you very much indeed.

Mary Robinson, the former president of Ireland, served as the United Nations high commissioner for human rights for five years.

GLORIA STEINEM

Wellesley College, 1993

I don't know about you, but I am incurably sentimental about commencements.

For one thing, they are a time when hopes are set free with so much future before us that hopes can be infinite. For another, all the diverse parts of this community are together—not just for the last time, but perhaps for the only time. I thank them all for letting me share it:

- President Nan Keohane, whose leadership will be so missed in the future—and yet whose impact on her new university, so appropriately called Duke, we can hardly wait to see;
- Skilled administrators and wise trustees—plus their friends, family, and significant others;
- Faculty with tenure, faculty without tenure—including international women's studies professor Jennifer Schirmer, whose student support has filled my mailbox;
- Parents and families of graduates, stepparents and chosen families of graduates—and everyone else who gave moral support and help to pay the bills;
- Lovers of graduates—you know who you are;
- Staff who fed, cleaned, housed, typed, and supported this class into being—including setting up this ceremony;

- Past graduates, future graduates, never-going-to-be graduates, and anyone else who, like me, is here because they're addicted to the poignancy of graduations;
- And most important, each and every member of the unique Class of 1993.

Davis Scholars who proved once again that women are the one group who grows more radical with age, and traditional students who are nontraditional in everything but age; students who hung out at Schneider Center or C.E. House, at memorial rock, Harambee House, or The Hoop; those who went to Hillary's Inaugural party and those who didn't, and yes, even those who voted for George Bush; those who thought the Nation of Islam text should be taught, those who didn't, and those who weren't sure; those who thought Wellesley chose them by mistake, and those who always knew they should be at Wellesley; students from Mezcla and the Asian Association, from the welfare rolls and the Blue Book, who took courses at MIT or Spelman, who qualified for athletic teams or championships for sitting still and reading—in other words, to everyone in this class, which represents the glorious and growing diversity of Wellesley, I say: You are a great motive for me—and for all of us here—to live a very long life. If we're really programmed to live up to one hundred thirty years, as geneticists now say, you inspire me to try. I want to see what you do in the world, for you're going to accomplish so much more than we did. After all, you're smarter and younger.

Even in your very first year on this campus, I remember reading some of you quoted in the national press. You were already having to defend your views on the great Barbara Bush controversy. "Would the husband of Margaret Thatcher be invited to Oxford?" "Would Harvard's commencement speaker be Mr. Sandra Day O'Connor?"

In your sophomore year, the Berlin Wall came down, Russian citizens thought about voting choice for the first time in history, and the power blocs of the world shifted in a way that outdated every textbook; yet some internal walls still wouldn't come down. A chaplain could be a woman, for instance, a great step forward from my day, when not only God but all his representatives were supposed to look like the ruling class—but for some, a chaplain still couldn't be a lesbian.

By the next year, Rodney King and the Los Angeles rebellion had become a flashpoint for all who were powerless or empathized with the powerless; the long-suppressed ethnic tensions of eastern Europe erupted; and we had gone to war against the Middle Eastern dictator we had helped to create. As if in a faint echo of world tensions, biased graffiti appeared here, too. But in this community, there were speak-outs, teach-ins, peaceful demonstrations, and empathetic efforts to cross barriers. Take those skills with you. The world needs them.

And then suddenly in your senior year, with the stroke of an election, this country's hopes have been raised. The spirit of twelve Reagan/Bush years were characterized by one newspaper cartoonist this way: Reagan, in a Western hat, saying, "A gun in every holster, a pregnant woman in every home, make America a man again." The spirit of the Clinton years has thus far been characterized—even if also cartoonized—by a more equal partnership between a man and a woman than this country has ever seen at the top—or much of anywhere. And of course, Hillary Rodham Clinton is one of your own. First a copresident, then a president. Who knows, perhaps that first president will be one of you.

Yet at the same time, the world has been forced to recognize rape as a war crime by the rape camps of Bosnia, and a doctor in Florida was murdered for offering poor women reproductive freedom.

It's hard to imagine any class that has experienced more world-transforming events while getting a degree. To your credit, you have taken on many of these events on campus instead of retreating into an "Ivory Tower." I know from talking with you that you have learned that conflicts make you strong, and diversity multiplies everyone's learning.

But no commencement speaker can resist giving advice—certainly I can't. There are so many things I wish I had known on the day of my own commencement into independent life. Here are a few, on the off chance that they're helpful.

First, I wish I had known that an education is not a thing one gets, but a lifelong process. It took me twenty years to recover from my own college years, for it took me that long to realize how incomplete they had been. Fortunately, more of your courses have looked at the world as if women mattered—and thus you are far more likely to know that you matter.

But I look at, say, your president's name, Nannerl, and I wonder: How many of us know about Mozart's older sister, whose name was also Nannerl, and whom Mozart said was the really talented one.

Or I think of the ground underneath our feet right now, and I wonder how many of us study the sophisticated Native American cultures that once flourished here and throughout this continent; some with councils of grandmothers who chose the leaders and made decisions of war and peace; some with democratic forms to which our Constitution owes more than it does to ancient Greece.

I wonder how many of us were taught that slavery was the

forced importation of unskilled labor, when it was also a brain drain, with a conscious effort to steal experts in, say, the cultivation of rice.

And sometimes, I wonder if we can uproot the spirals of violence in this country at all, unless we admit and study their origins in the very settling of our country, in the ideas of "masculinity" and "femininity" that have imprinted our ideas of what human beings can be.

Just as violence and abuse in one person's childhood repeats itself until its truth is admitted and healed, so I sometimes wonder if violence and abuse in the beginning of a country's life must be truly admitted and studied before it can be healed. And I wonder why we don't study the clear correlation between child-rearing methods and forms of government; between routine physical abuse of children and growing up to believe one must be either the victim or the victimizer—there's no other choice. Perhaps we should have a motto: "The only form of one's control is how we raise our children." Those are just a few thoughts to tantalize you into a continuing education.

Second, I wish I had better understood the importance of process itself. Process is all.

For instance, the ends don't justify the means. The means are the ends. Unless the means we use reflect the values we hope to achieve, we can never achieve them. For instance, no one can give us power. If we aren't part of the process of taking it, we won't be strong enough to use it. For instance, a person who has experienced something is always more expert in it than the experts. For instance, the Golden Rule, written by and for men, needs reversal to be valuable to many women. Yes, it's important to treat others as we ourselves would wish to be treated. But for us women the challenge is to treat ourselves as well as we treat others. After all, who wants a Golden Rule administered by a masochist?

And finally, I wish I'd known the life-giving importance of support from other women. You've learned that in these years at Wellesley. Some of you have told me that you fear its loss. Well, refuse to lose it. Wherever you go, make sure that you have a small group of women with whom you meet often and regularly; women with whom you can share support, jokes, values, dreams, and activism to advance those values and dreams.

I hope men here realize this is not exclusionary; that we join together with men, too. But women, whatever our race or class, our sexuality or ethnicity, are the one subordinate group that doesn't have a country. Indeed, we will never have a country, which is good; for it makes us antinationalistic and subversive. But we also don't have a neighborhood. Most of us don't even have a bar. Many of us are treated unequally, even within our own loved families.

So until we have a truly equal world, we will need to come together in small groups to form psychic countries and alternate families of women. As long as we are spending some part of our lives in a woman-hating culture, we will need a woman-loving group to counter it; just as racism requires a racial pride to counter its bias.

It is only such support that lets us know we are not crazy, the system is crazy; that keeps us from feeling aberrant, self-blaming, alone; that keeps us from internalizing the values that devalue us.

With such regular, built-in, small groups, personal/political support, there is no end to the dreams we can nurture.

Since there can be no revolution without poetry—as Emma Goldman said, music and dancing—I'll leave you with my favorite poem by Marge Piercy. It explains why one twig can be broken, but a bundle of twigs cannot; why you must learn from the support of these college years to seek out supportive women, wherever you are.

Alone, you can fight, you can refuse, you can
take what revenge you can
but they roll over you.
But two people fighting
back to back can cut through
a mob, a snake-dancing file
can break a cordon, an army
can meet an army.
Two people can keep each other
sane, can give support, conviction,
love, massage, hope, sex
Three people are a delegation,
a committee, a wedge. With four
you can play bridge and start
an organization. With six
you can rent a whole house,
eat pie for dinner with no
seconds, and hold a fund raising party.
A dozen make a demonstration.
A hundred fill a hall.
A thousand have solidarity and your own newsletter;
ten thousand, power and your own paper;
a hundred thousand, your own media;
ten million, your own country.
It goes on—one at a time,
It starts when you care
to act, it starts when you do
it again after they said no,

it starts when you say We
and know who you mean, and each
day you mean one more.

And remember: If your dreams weren't already real within us, you could not even dream them.

Gloria Steinem, founder of Ms. *magazine and renowned feminist, has been a spokesperson for women's rights since the 1970s.*

WRITERS

Good novels are written by people who are not frightened.

—*George Orwell*

EDWARD ALBEE

Choate Rosemary Hall, 1999

The Wound of Self-Awareness

L et me tell you a little about me. Back in 1941–42, I was at the Lawrenceville School and I managed to get myself thrown out. I didn't do anything terrible. I didn't burn the chapel down. It was a kind of passive resistance. I didn't want to be there and so I didn't go to classes.

My family decided that I probably needed a little discipline. Instead of sending me to an educational institution, [they] sent me to Valley Forge Military Academy in Pennsylvania. The courses were compulsory; no electives there. I managed to get thrown out of Valley Forge Military Academy. No easy task at such a terminal joint.

My family decided to give me one more chance at education and so I managed to get myself into Choate, but my grades were so terrible I had to go to summer school up at Hill House so I could start at Choate. I almost got thrown out of Choate my second week of summer school when three or four of my friends and I climbed down the ivy (I noticed there is no longer any ivy up there on Hill House) and went to Meriden to a saloon and were soon interrupted by some very nice Choate teacher who brought us back and did not have us dismissed.

They taught me two things here at Choate. They taught me how to do whatever I wanted to [do] and make a fool of myself as much as I wanted to. I acted all the time, was on the debating team and prize speaking team. I ran the classical music radio station and was managing editor of *The Lit,* filling it with my own work, of course. I painted; I won second prize in a school art contest. I managed to do nothing terribly well and made a fool of myself. Great, great training for what is called "adult life." [But] they also taught me something enormously important here. They taught me that the function of a formal education is to teach yourself how to go on educating yourself once you're finished with your formal education. A graduation is merely a beginning of your education.

Things have changed a lot at Choate since I was here fifty-some years ago. Choate has wisely and inevitably become more inclusive and more welcoming of people from diverse backgrounds—essential for an important educational institution to survive.

The most important thing, perhaps, that has been done to you the graduating class and done to those of you who will graduate in years to come is that Choate has wounded each of you—fatally and decisively. You have been wounded into a kind of self-awareness—an awareness of what your responsibilities are to yourself and to other people—a wound that is never going to heal. If you don't pay proper attention to that wound, you're going to be very, very unhappy people. The wound is self-awareness that your responsibilities to yourself are to fulfill your own destinies, your own dreams, and your own desires in the ways that are best and inevitable to you.

I am convinced that one should not go to college until one is thirty years old. Go out there for ten or twelve years. Find out something about the world. How can you possibly know at the age of seventeen, eighteen, and nineteen what you want to do for the rest of your life? How can you possibly know that? But since you're all going to be going to college next year, you're going to be going with this profound wound of self-awareness that you are at college in order to learn more about being the person that you want to be.

I read a discouraging thing in the *New York Times* a couple of years ago. Several thousand graduating college students were asked why they had gone to college, and 75 percent of them said [it was] to get a good job and make a lot of money. That is not why you are going to college. That may be an incidental occurrence to you. You're going to college to continue your education and to continue your self-awareness.

You have the responsibility to be socially responsible and socially aware, to be aware that you have received an education that very, very few other people in this country are receiving. You also have a responsibility to this thing we call democracy—a responsibility to participate in the politics of your society. I have been watching with despair as more and more college students are abandoning political involvement and political responsibility. How else without your involvement can this extraordinary, peacefully evolving revolutionary society called the United States proceed if we become a totally passive society? If we lose faith in our ability to make profound changes, then democracy, being an enormously fragile thing, will conceivably vanish. You must involve yourself politically; you must involve yourself socially; and you must do only those things that when you get to the end of your life you can say to yourself, "Yeah, I'm glad I did it that way; I'm glad I did it for myself."

This is commencement. Commence!

The author of Who's Afraid of Virginia Woolf?, *Edward Albee debuted as a playwright in 1959. He has been awarded both Tony Awards and Pulitzer Prizes.*

SHERMAN ALEXIE

University of Washington, Seattle, 2003

Oh, this is great. I'm nervous. I haven't spoken to this many people before. And I didn't actually go through my graduation ceremony, so this is new for me as well. I felt like Rudy coming out of the walkway over there.

The only reason I agreed to do this is if they would let me wear a really cool hat.

I'm really happy to be here. I'd like to thank the University of Washington administration, faculty, and staff for asking me to give this commencement address. And, as you heard, I will be joining the faculty next year, so this is sort of my first official lecture. I'll try to make it educational, inspiring, humorous, and very, very brief.

Like you heard, I am a graduate of Washington State University. I'm a Cougar. You know . . . [SINGS COUGARS FIGHT SONG]. So I feel a little bit like a spy today. But in the sprit of full disclosure I must tell you that I'm only a Cougar by accident.

Sixteen years ago, in the summer of 1987, I moved from Spokane to Seattle and transferred from Gonzaga in the hopes of attending the University of Washington. But while working at a sandwich shop, a Hoagie's Corner just down the street here, on graveyard shift, I was robbed at knifepoint. The morning after the robbery I filled out the police report, did the little sketch, packed up my car with everything I owned, which wasn't much, and then, with a broken heart, I fled back to eastern Washington. I was a reservation Dorothy defeated by the Emerald City.

It was in Pullman that I became a writer. Now, I hadn't originally planned to become a writer. I wanted to be a pediatrician, so when I heard the award up here [given to a UW pediatrician] I was really jealous of her. And I was also jealous of that 3.98 grade point average, Brooks [referring to Brooks Aaron Minor, who received a medal for "most distinguished academic record" in the graduating class]. Do you think he's really angry with the two A minuses he got? You know he lies in bed at night and . . . you know . . . *Those bastard teachers.*

I was a chemistry major originally, with a pre-med emphasis. But I couldn't handle human anatomy lab. I kept fainting. And during surgery it might be okay to leave the occasional sponge or scalpel inside your patient, but it's not very good to leave your whole head and shoulders area there.

So, with a broken heart and with my dreams dashed, right—and that's what happens to us when we come into college with all these ideas of who we're going to be, and that changes rapidly. And mine changed rapidly, and I had to give up the idea of becoming a doctor—that dream.

And so I considered my options. I was a smart Indian kid, a Native American kid. And smart Indian kids are supposed to be tribal saviors. We're supposed to be Jesus. And, in a capitalistic and secular society, you get to be Jesus by becoming a doctor or lawyer. And now I couldn't be a doctor because of the whole fainting goat syndrome I had apparently contracted. I couldn't be a lawyer, because I'm an Indian and I've met lots of lawyers, and all they ever wanted me to do was sign treaties. So I thought, okay, I can't be a doctor or a lawyer, the two most lucrative professions in the country, so what's the third most lucrative profession in the country—and it's poetry.

My parents were really, really happy about that career choice. I mean, the thing is, I was the first person in my family to ever go to college, let alone graduate from college. And there have only been a handful of Spokane Indians who have ever graduated from any college. Far less than one percent of all college graduates this year are Native American. We are rare, rare, rare, we Indians with college degrees. And even rarer are those Indians who get the commencement addresses.

So, you Native Americans in the crowd who are graduating, will you please stand up?

[THE NATIVE AMERICAN STUDENTS STAND.]

I know how hard it is, baby! Congratulations!

Despite my special stature as a rare Indian, I didn't go through my graduation ceremony. And I regret that all the time. I didn't participate in this amazing and sacred ceremony. So I want to thank all of you graduates today for allowing me to be a part of *your* amazing and sacred ceremony. And to acknowledge all the friends and family here who are also here to celebrate and to participate in this amazing and sacred ceremony.

And I really and especially want to honor a very distinguished group of graduates. And I'm speaking of you men and women out there who are the first in your family to go to college and the first in your family to graduate from college. Will you please stand up?

[HUNDREDS OF GRADUATES STAND.]

I'm talking about social, educational, political, and economic pioneers. And I'm a pioneer too, which is a really odd thing for an Indian to be. And us pioneers, we've all been able to transcend real and imaginary barriers of race, class, and country, only because of the universities we've attended, because of this university, because of the education we've received, and because of the special and dedicated attentions of college administrators, teachers, and staff.

And all of you Husky pioneers have certainly triumphed as individuals, but you've also done something equally important. You've created a map for your children to follow. And whether you come from a mining town or a farm town, from a reservation or a barrio, from inner-city Chicago, Illinois, or inner-city Burien, you've also made a map for your neighbors and for your tribes to follow.

And that's what a university can give us. It can give us freedom. It can give us mobility. It can give us access. It can fill us with such curiosity that we are forced to explore the furthest reaches of the world, and more importantly, the furthest reaches of our souls.

And isn't that what we truly want from our teachers? You're going to forget most of the details you learned here. I don't remember anything from high school. And not much more from college. But your soul has expanded here, and it will continue to expand after you leave here. But only if you continue to be voracious and curious. If you continue to make this day and every day as sacred and amazing.

This universe is an amazing and sacred place. The idea of university is amazing and sacred. As John Sexton, the president of New York University, has noted, there are only eighty-five human institutions that have been in continuous operation for more than five hundred years, and seventy-five of those human institutions are universities, beginning with Alazar University in Egypt.

So when we talk about the idea of university, about this special place of knowledge and learning, we are talking about something so human and so enduring and so necessary. It is at universities where we are the best we can possibly be as human beings, as citizens of the world, as citizens of this state, this country and city.

Look around you, and you will see graduates from dozens of countries. Look at the color of the people around you. We're in some gigantic Crayola box right now. You've got the beige section over there, and the mauve section over here, and the siennas over there in the back. I can guarantee you, graduates, for most of you, your lives will never be this diverse again. You will never experience this diversity of race and religion, of politics and identity, of geography and spirit, of vocations and avocations.

Now, our public school systems, our universities, our high schools, they often get the blame for our social problems. And our Supreme Court and our government are now considering, and will always consider, legal cases that can fundamentally change the way our institutions are structured. But where else in this country are the ideals of democracy best represented than at universities? Where else is there a better chance for the poor in hope to become rich in ideas? Where else is there a better chance for the marginalized and forgotten to become passionate and fully active citizens? Where else is there a better chance for the oppressed to break free of their chains and invent a new way to be free?

Hell, it's here at college that most of you have already met the person you're going to marry. And the rest of you will spend the rest of your lives looking back at college thinking about that person that you probably should have married.

I know you all understand the importance of this day. But I want you to understand the importance of every day. A few weeks ago, I taught my two-year-old son how to say "Carpe diem," which, as you know, in Latin means "Seize the day." Now, my little son loves to talk to strangers. So, I want you all to imagine a two-year-old Indian boy running around Seattle screaming at strangers, "Carpe diem! Carpe diem! Carpe diem!"

Two weeks ago at a Seattle city park, while on a field trip with our eldest son's kindergarten class, my two-year-old ran up to a stranger, a young woman who was maybe twenty years old, and he smiled at her and screamed, "Carpe diem!" This young woman stared incredulously at him, at me, at him, at me. She couldn't believe what was going on, and she asked who taught him that. And I said I taught him that. But then I thought, no, he's two years old; he already knows how to seize the day.

My son is always in the present, always eating, always moving, always voracious and passionate. He learns a dozen new words every damn day. How many of you learn a dozen words every damn day? I haven't learned a dozen words in the last decade. So I didn't teach my son how to seize the day. I've only given him the vocabulary to describe a philosophy he already espouses. So . . . Carpe diem! Carpe diem! Carpe diem!

I know at the end of this commencement address I'm supposed to give you advice. I'm supposed to challenge you. I'm supposed to tell you to go out there and change the world. And I don't know if you are going to do any of that, and I don't know if any of you are interested in doing any of that. But I have hopes and prayers invested in all of you total strangers. And I hope all of you have hopes and prayers invested in all of the other total strangers in this stadium, in this city, in this world and country. In fact, I hope all of us strangers here love all the other strangers enough to want to make the world a more educated and imaginative place for all of us to live in.

We've been confronted with old problems, and we've met them with old solutions. And I'm hoping somewhere out there is somebody with brand-new ideas.

So there you go. I'm not really interested in how much you love your neighbors. That's easy. There's nothing easier than loving your neighbor. I'm more interested in how well you love total strangers. It's that love for strangers that will make you an educated, literate, passionate, imaginative, and special human being.

Once again I congratulate all of you. Those of you who are continuing marvelous family traditions, and those of you who have started a new and marvelous family tradition, I wish you all well in your various journeys.

Thank you.

Writer Sherman Alexie, a Spokane/Coeur d'Alene Indian, is the award-winning author of numerous novels, short stories, poems, and screenplays.

NORA EPHRON

Wellesley College, 1996

P resident Walsh, trustees, faculty, friends, noble parents, and dear Class of 1996, I am so proud of you.
Thank you for asking me to speak to you today. I had a
wonderful time trying to imagine who had been ahead of me
on the list and had said no; I was positive you'd have to have
gone to Martha Stewart first. And I meant to call her to see
what she would have said, but I forgot. She would probably
be up here telling you how to turn your lovely black robes
into tents. I will try to be at least as helpful, if not quite as
specific as that.

I'm very conscious of how easy it is to let people down on
a day like this, because I remember my own graduation from
Wellesley very, very well, I am sorry to say. The speaker was
Santha Rama Rau, who was a woman writer, and I was going
to be a woman writer. And in fact, I had spent four years at
Wellesley going to lectures by women writers hoping that I
would be the beneficiary of some terrific secret—which
I never was. And now here I was at graduation, under
these very trees, absolutely terrified. Something was over.
Something safe and protected. And something else was about
to begin. I was heading off to New York and I was sure that I
would live there forever and never meet anyone and end up
dying one of those New York deaths where no one even notices

you're missing until the smell drifts into the hallway weeks later. And I sat here thinking, "Okay, Santha, this is my last chance for a really terrific secret, lay it on me," and she spoke about the need to place friendship over love of country, which I must tell you had never crossed my mind one way or the other.

I want to tell you a little bit about my class, the Class of 1962. When we came to Wellesley in the fall of 1958, there was an article in the *Harvard Crimson* about the women's colleges, one of those stupid mean little articles full of stereotypes, like girls at Bryn Mawr wear black. We were girls then, by the way, Wellesley girls. How long ago was it? It was so long ago that while I was here, Wellesley actually threw six young women out for lesbianism. It was so long ago that we had curfews. It was so long ago that if you had a boy in your room, you had to leave the door open six inches, and if you closed the door you had to put a sock on the doorknob. In my class of, I don't know, maybe three hundred seventy-five young women, there were six Asians and five blacks. There was a strict quota on the number of Jews. Tuition was $2,000 a year, and in my junior year it was raised to $2,250 and my parents practically had a heart attack.

How long ago? If you needed an abortion, you drove to a gas station in Union, New Jersey, with $500 in cash in an envelope and you were taken, blindfolded, to a motel room and operated on without an anesthetic. On the lighter side, and as you no doubt read in the *New York Times Magazine* and were flabbergasted to learn, there were the posture pictures. We not only took off most of our clothes to have our posture pictures taken, we took them off without ever even thinking, *This is weird, why are we doing this?* Not only that, we had also had speech therapy—I was told I had a New

Jersey accent I really ought to do something about, which was a shock to me since I was from Beverly Hills, California, and had never set foot in the state of New Jersey. Not only that, we were required to take a course called Fundamentals— Fundies—where we actually were taught how to get in and out of the backseat of the car. Some of us were named things like Winkie. We all parted our hair in the middle. How long ago was it? It was so long ago that among the things that I honestly cannot conceive of life without, that had not yet been invented: pantyhose, lattes, Advil, pasta (there was no pasta then, there was only spaghetti and macaroni)—I sit here writing this speech on a computer next to a touch-tone phone with an answering machine and a Rolodex, there are several CDs on my desk, a bottle of Snapple, there are felt-tip pens and an electric pencil sharpener . . . well, you get the point, it was a long time ago.

Anyway, as I was saying, the *Crimson* had this snippy article which said that Wellesley was a school for tunicata—tunicata apparently being small fish who spend the first part of their lives frantically swimming around the ocean floor exploring their environment, and the second part of their lives just lying there breeding. It was mean and snippy, but it had the horrible ring of truth, it was one of those do-not-ask-for-whom-the-bell-tolls things, and it burned itself into our brains. Years later, at my twenty-fifth reunion, one of my classmates mentioned it, and everyone remembered what tunicata were, word for word.

My class went to college in the era when you got a master's degree in teaching because it was "something to fall back on" in the worst-case scenario, the worst-case scenario being that no one married you and you actually had to go to work. As this same classmate said at our reunion, "Our education was a dress rehearsal for a life we never led." Isn't that the saddest line? We weren't meant to have futures, we were meant to marry them. We weren't meant to have politics, or careers that mattered, or opinions, or lives; we were meant to marry them. If you wanted to be an architect, you married an architect. *Non ministrare sed ministrari*—you know the old joke, not to be ministers but to be ministers' wives.

I've written about my years at Wellesley, and I don't want to repeat myself any more than is necessary. But I do want to retell one anecdote from the piece I did about my tenth Wellesley reunion. I'll tell it a little differently for those of you who read it. Which was that, during my junior year, when I was engaged for a very short period of time, I thought I might transfer to Barnard my senior year. I went to see my class dean and she said to me, "Let me give you some advice. You've worked so hard at Wellesley, when you marry, take a year off. Devote yourself to your husband and your marriage." Of course it was a stunning piece of advice to give me, because I'd always intended to work after college. My mother was a career woman, and all of us, her four daughters, grew up understanding that the question, "What do you want to be when you grow up?" was as valid for girls as for boys. Take a year off being a wife. I always wondered what I was supposed to do in that year. Iron? I repeated the story for years, as proof that Wellesley wanted its graduates to be merely housewives. But I turned out to be wrong, because years later I met another Wellesley graduate who had been as hell-bent on domesticity as I had been on a career. And she had gone to the same dean with the same problem, and the dean had said to her, "Don't have children right away. Take a year to work." And so I saw that what Wellesley wanted was for us to avoid the extremes. To be instead, that thing in the middle. A lady. We were to take the fabulous education we had received here and use it to preside at the dinner table or at a committee meeting, and when two people disagreed we would be intelligent enough to step in and point out the remarkable similarities between their two opposing positions. We were to spend our lives making nice.

Many of my classmates did exactly what they were supposed to when they graduated from Wellesley, and some of them, by the way, lived happily ever after. But many of them didn't. All sorts of things happened that no one expected. They needed money, so they had to work. They got divorced, so they had to work. They were bored witless, so they had to work. The women's movement came along and made harsh value judgments about their lives—judgments that caught them by surprise, because they were doing what they were supposed to be doing, weren't they? The rules had changed, they were caught in some kind of strange time warp. They had never intended to be the heroines of their own lives, they'd intended to be—what?—First Ladies, I guess, First Ladies in the lives of big men. They ended up feeling like victims. They ended up, and this is really sad, thinking that their years in college were the best years of their lives.

Why am I telling you this? It was a long time ago, right? Things have changed, haven't they? Yes, they have. But I mention it because I want to remind you of the undertow, of the specific gravity. American society has a remarkable ability to resist change, or to take whatever change has taken place and attempt to make it go away. Things are different for you than they were for us. Just the fact that you chose to come to a single-sex college makes you smarter than we were—we came because it's what you did in those days—and the college you are graduating from is a very different place. All sorts of things caused Wellesley to change, but it did change, and today it's a place that understands its obligations to women in today's world. The women's movement has made a huge difference, too, particularly for young women like you. There are women doctors and women lawyers. There are anchorwomen, although most of them are blonde. But at the same time, the pay differential between men and women has barely changed. In my business, the movie business, there are many more women directors, but it's just as hard to make a movie about women as it ever was, and look at the parts the Oscar-nominated actresses played this year: hooker, hooker, hooker, hooker, and nun. It's 1996, and you are graduating from Wellesley in the Year of the Wonderbra. The Wonderbra is not a step forward for women. Nothing that hurts that much is a step forward for women.

What I'm saying is, don't delude yourself that the powerful cultural values that wrecked the lives of so many of my classmates have vanished from the earth. Don't let the *New York Times* article about the brilliant success of Wellesley graduates in the business world fool you—there's still a glass ceiling. Don't let the number of women in the workforce trick you— there are still lots of magazines devoted almost exclusively to making perfect casseroles and turning various things into tents.

Don't underestimate how much antagonism there is toward women and how many people wish we could turn the clock back. One of the things people always say to you if you get upset is, don't take it personally—but listen hard to what's going on and, please, I beg you, take it personally. Understand: Every attack on Hillary Clinton for not knowing her place is an attack on you. Underneath almost all those attacks are the words: Get back, get back to where you once belonged. When Elizabeth Dole pretends that she isn't serious about her career, that is an attack on you. The acquittal of O. J. Simpson is an attack on you. Any move to limit abortion rights is an attack on you—whether or not you believe in abortion. The fact that Clarence Thomas is sitting on the Supreme Court today is an attack on you.

Above all, be the heroine of your life, not the victim. Because you don't have the alibi my class had—this is one of the great achievements and mixed blessings you inherit: Unlike us, you can't say nobody told you there were other options. Your education is a dress rehearsal for a life that is yours to lead. Twenty-five years from now, you won't have as easy a time making excuses as my class did. You won't be able to blame the deans, or the culture, or anyone else: You will have no one to blame but yourselves. Whoa.

So what are you going to do? This is the season when a clutch of successful women—who have it all—give speeches to women like you and say, to be perfectly honest, you can't have it all. Maybe young women don't wonder whether they can have it all any longer, but in case you are wondering, of course you can have it all. What are you going to do? Everything, is my guess. It will be a little messy, but embrace the mess. It will be complicated, but rejoice in the complications. It will not be anything like what you think it will be like, but surprises are good for you. And don't be frightened: You can always change your mind. I know: I've had four careers and three husbands. And this is something else I want to tell you, one of the hundreds of things I didn't know when I was sitting here so many years ago: You are not going to be you, fixed and immutable you, forever. We have a game we play when we're waiting for tables in restaurants, where you have to write the five things that describe yourself on a piece of paper. When I was your age, I would have put: ambitious, Wellesley graduate, daughter, Democrat, single. Ten years later

175

not one of those five things turned up on my list. I was: journalist, feminist, New Yorker, divorced, funny. Today not one of those five things turns up in my list: writer, director, mother, sister, happy. Whatever those five things are for you today, they won't make the list in ten years—not that you still won't be some of those things, but they won't be the five most important things about you. Which is one of the most delicious things available to women, and more particularly to women than to men, I think. It's slightly easier for us to shift, to change our minds, to take another path. Yogi Berra, the former New York Yankee who made a specialty of saying things that were famously maladroit, quoted himself at a recent commencement speech he gave. "When you see a fork in the road," he said, "take it." Yes, it's supposed to be a joke, but as someone said in a movie I made, "Don't laugh, this is my life," this is the life many women lead: Two paths diverge in a wood, and we get to take them both. It's another of the nicest things about being women; we can do that. Did I say it was hard? Yes, but let me say it again so that none of you can ever say the words, nobody said it was so hard. But it's also incredibly interesting. You are so lucky to have that life as an option.

Whatever you choose, however many roads you travel, I hope that you choose not to be a lady. I hope you will find some way to break the rules and make a little trouble out there. And I also hope that you will choose to make some of that trouble on behalf of women. Thank you. Good luck. The first act of your life is over. Welcome to the best years of your lives.

Nora Ephron is known as an essayist, novelist, screenwriter, and director. Her essay collections have been best-sellers, and she has received three Academy Award nominations for best original screenplay.

MICHAEL IGNATIEFF

Whitman College, 2004

Living Fearlessly in a Fearful World

Y ou have done me a great honor and I accept it with gratitude. It is a pleasure for my wife and me to be part of the Whitman community today.

A speech on graduation day should be short and to the point. I know only too well that I am a warm-up act. The main event—the moment you are waiting for—comes later, when you step up and get your degrees and you pose with your loved ones, the good people who sacrificed to get you to this moment, the doubters who never thought you'd make it, the quiet heroes who had faith in you when you didn't have any yourself. It would be foolish of me to delay this moment of joy and recognition too long. Let me just offer you my heartfelt congratulations, especially to those among you who are the first members of your family to get a college degree. Try to make sure that this moment becomes a tradition in your family, for your children and your children's children.

Do remember Whitman College when you leave. I have taught in the university systems of Canada, the United Kingdom, and France, and from my experience, American higher education is the best in the world, especially because of the strength of its private liberal arts colleges. One reason for their strength is the astounding generosity of their alumni, their willingness to give back to the institutions that gave them their chance. Please continue that fine tradition.

Having given you a piece of financial advice, let me move on to the staple fare of any commencement address: moral advice. No person of my advanced years, given this honor, can avoid succumbing to the temptation to give advice to an audience held captive like this, and I shall succumb like all the others.

My theme is living fearlessly in a fearful world. Living fearlessly is not the same thing as never being afraid. It's good to be afraid occasionally. Fear is a great teacher. What's not good is living in fear, allowing fear to dictate your choices, allowing fear to define who you are. Living fearlessly means standing up to fear, taking its measure, refusing to let it shape and define your life. Living fearlessly means taking risks, taking gambles, not playing it safe. It means refusing to take "no" for an answer when you are sure that the answer should have been "yes." It means refusing to settle for less than what is your due, what is yours by right, what is yours by the sweat of your labor and your effort. To those of you who have had to struggle to get here, who sometimes doubted that you were going to get through, remember this: You have already come too far to settle for less than the best.

Why am I talking about fear at a moment like this? Because your adult life is really about to begin: jobs, professions, marriages, relationships, children, responsibilities, burdens, worries, and yes, fear. Fear that you are not good enough to make the grade. Fear that you haven't got what it takes to carry the burden. Fear that you can't meet the expectations of all those people watching you today as you step up and accept your degree.

Fight the fear. Remember, the most important thing about a

life is that it is yours and nobody else's. You cannot live a life for the sake of your family, your parents, your brothers, your sisters, your children. A life without duty to these loved ones would not be a good life, but a life lived entirely to meet their expectations is not a good life. It is the ones who love us most who put the fear into us, who burden us with expectations and responsibilities we feel unable to meet. So we need to say, "This is our life, not yours, and we are going to do this our way."

One of the greatest feelings in life is the conviction that you have lived the life you wanted to live—with the rough and the smooth, the good and the bad—but yours, shaped by your own choices, and not someone else's. To do that, you have to conquer fear, get control of the expectations that drive your life, and decide what goals are truly yours to achieve.

Doing this—making sure that the life you lead is the one you want to lead, and that you are prepared to lead it this way, whatever anybody says—is never easy. It's not made any easier by the times we live in.

We live in a fearful time, perhaps the most fearful times for the United States since the Vietnam War. When I graduated, it was June of 1969, and Americans were dying in hundreds every week in Southeast Asia. Today as you graduate, young Americans are dying every day in Iraq. Like Vietnam, Iraq divides Americans, and so it should. America is a democracy as well as a community of sacrifice. But sacrifice is only acceptable in a democracy if its rationale is supported by a majority of citizens. Questioning the rationale for war is not unpatriotic. Democratic debate does not demean the sacrifice of brave men and women: Indeed, democratic debate—the lifeblood of freedom— is what the bravery is supposed to be defending.

As young citizens, you should not be bystanders in this

debate. This war concerns you because its course and its outcome will determine your security for years to come. The conduct of the war defines America as a nation: its moral reputation at home and abroad. So in this election year, when so many young Americans don't bother to vote, please don't listen to the cynics who say it doesn't matter how you vote or whether you vote. Please don't listen to the people who say, "I don't know whom to believe, so I'm staying home on Election Day." Take part. Get involved. Become a precinct captain. Drive people to the polls. Canvass for your candidate. Raise money for people who run for political office. Be a good citizen, because that is what it actually means to be a good American.

Being a good citizen and being a good American also mean looking fair and square at disagreeable realities. Being a good citizen means living in truth. Living in truth is hard. It's hard to face the truth about ourselves, and it's hard to face the truth about our country. But we know that living in truth is better than living a lie.

We are living a moment of truth in Iraq, a moment in which we have to look fair and square at disagreeable realities, in which we have to look at ourselves. The pictures from Abu Ghraib prison are a kind of mirror in which we have to look at ourselves and ask: What kind of people did this? How did this become possible? Could I have done a thing like this to those people?

We do need to ask ourselves, as a society, as a free people, how we came to this pass. Those soldiers were acting in the name of America, and they disgraced its name. We have to ask who authorized them to do so. Who should take responsibility here?

We need answers to these questions, and we need to take responsibility as citizens to get answers, and have accountability established, right up the chain of command if need be, so that we do not go here again as a country.

Responsibility is a key element of living fearlessly. Taking responsibility: not being afraid to carry the can, when the can has to be carried by someone; not being afraid to demand that someone take responsibility, when everyone is ducking it. It's hard to be responsible. It's hard to take responsibility. But it is what it means to be an adult and a citizen.

I don't like watching leaders who won't take responsibility for what happened in those prisons. I don't like ordinary soldiers carrying the can for errors of judgment and errors of command that went to the top of the chain of command. We deserve better from our leaders. We deserve better of those who serve in our name.

We need to acknowledge that the United States is a great country, but it is currently feared and hated by millions of people throughout the world. It is hated for being what it is: the most successful and powerful country in the history of the world. It is hated for what it does, for the policies of its government, in all administrations. As young adults, you have to take responsibility to do something about this hatred, this intense dislike for everything that America is and does that is sweeping through the Middle East and Europe. You may think it is undeserved. You may think it is unfair. You would be right. But that doesn't matter. The fact is, America is as unpopular as at any time in the last half century.

This gives us reason to fear. There are people out there who want to kill us and destroy our way of life. We have to live with this. It is a fact of life nowadays, like the weather.

There is only one thing we can do about this: live the way we are supposed to live, as our Constitution commands us to, with dignity and respect for all. Being an American is not easy.

It is hard. We are required to keep some serious promises. We are judged by a high standard, one we crafted for ourselves in the founding documents of the republic, the ones that talk about the equality of all people, the ones that tell us that government is of the people, by the people, and for the people. We need to live by this, at home and abroad, and it is just about the only thing we can do to face the hatred of those who want to destroy us. Our best defense is to stay true to who we are. Our best defense is to refuse to live in fear of them, of ourselves, of anyone.

We have examples to guide us. America is constantly affording us proof that its people understand what it is to be a member of this particular democratic experiment. It is right to remember Army Specialist Joseph Darby and celebrate his fearlessness today. He is the young reservist in the 372nd Military Police Company who put the note under a superior's door detailing the abuse by fellow members of his unit. It was his disclosure that led to the uncovering of the worst scandal in American military history since the My Lai massacre.

Consider what he was up against: loyalty to his own unit; fear that he would not be believed; fear that his fellow unit members would take revenge if they found out, or ostracize him and his family. He risked himself, his career, and his good name to get the truth out. Because he saw something in Abu Ghraib that ashamed him as a human being and as an American. Something that made him afraid. Something that was wrong.

Thanks to his fearlessness, we are in the middle of a painful but essential moment of truth in righting our course in Iraq and the wider Middle East. Some voices are saying we are making too much of this. Some voices are calling on America to circle the wagons. Some are even saying that our enemies do worse, so we should respond in kind. The problem here is that this is America. This is a constitutional republic based on the rule of law and equal respect for all persons. We can't pretend that we can bend the rules any which way. We made the rules for ourselves. We have to live by them. Specialist Darby understood that. He is one of the fearless ones, someone who fought fear and doubt in order to tell a necessary, if painful, truth.

Not everyone is going to be a Specialist Darby. Your lives may not call for or require any special heroism. Yet all lives require an encounter with fear, a battle with an emotion that can carry us away from our true selves. So we need to remember heroic people's examples, so that we can live ordinary lives decently and in truth. My final word to you is this: In a fearful time, try to be one of the fearless ones. Thank you very much.

Michael Ignatieff is renowned internationally for his work as a commentator and author on moral, ethical, and political issues, and has taught at universities such as Oxford, Harvard, Cambridge, and the London School of Economics.

WALLY LAMB

"What Do Novelists Know?"

President Fainstein, Connecticut College trustees, faculty, and staff: Thank you for the invitation to speak today; it's my privilege to do so.

Fellow parents and elders of today's graduates: As one of the troubadours of our baby boomer generation, Joni Mitchell, used to sing, "We're captives on the carousel of time." My hope is that, as you listen to these reflections, they'll resonate with you and allow you to nod in recognition.

Finally, most especially, members of the Class of 2003: As you can see, I've lugged no weighty book of wisdom to this podium. I stand before you on your special day not with answers but with questions, and with an abridged history of my fifty-two-year-old trial-and-error American life as student, teacher, father, and fiction writer. So make of my words what you will, and also, please note that I've fired up the retro-rockets. Fasten your seat belts, everyone. We're about to blast backwards into the virtual past.

We'll try a short trip first. Look, we're here already; it's February of 2003. The Bush administration is hard-selling the case for invasion, Home Depot is selling out of duct tape and plastic sheeting, and on the front lawns of many American homes "No War on Iraq" signs are popping up through the snow like mutant crocuses. We're innocent, still, of the concept of "embedded" journalism and that new marketing slogan, "shock and awe"—but our initiation is upon us. Diplomacy is defunct, our leaders tell us. War is inevitable.

I'm in my office when a challenge arrives via Outlook Express. The novelist Dennis Lehane has drafted a petition to President Bush which acknowledges the tyranny of Saddam Hussein but asks that all diplomatic measures be exhausted before we risk ending the lives of innocent Iraqis and American military. Lehane invites fellow writers to sign.

Now, I want what Lehane wants, but I admit this to you, graduates: I blink. I walk around the office. Weigh the pros and cons of signing. There is, after all, the book buyer to consider; there's product waiting in the warehouse at Amazon.com. Like it or not, we're in an era of intolerance for dissenting opinion. The Dixie Chicks have yet to be beheaded, plucked, and rotisserie-roasted, but the White House has cancelled a literary event where antiwar poets were to speak. In the wake of social satirist Bill Maher's remarks about terrorism, the president's press secretary has warned that we must all watch what we say, and Maher has lost his television show. So maybe I shouldn't sign that petition, I think. Still, my kids are watching me, listening to me, studying my responses to the world, and I do not want to send them the message that they can speak their minds at the dinner table but they had better shut up once they get into the school cafeteria. This, after all, is America, where patriotism speaks in many different voices and need not nod mutely like a smiling bobble head. And so, along with one hundred fifty other writers, among them Julia Alvarez, Amy Tan, Richard Russo, and Stephen King, I sign the petition. It's published in the *New York Times* and the following day, another e-mail arrives, this one from a reporter for a different national newspaper. He wants to know what makes me think novelists know anything about war—why I assume fiction writers have any of the answers.

Hmm. Good question, Mr. Journalist. . . . Please note that I've turned on the seat belt sign. We're heading back to the year 1961.

Whether you've been here before or not, have a look. Dwight Eisenhower is moving out of the White House and John Kennedy's moving in. The space race is on, our astronauts chasing Soviet cosmonauts into the heavens, while back on terra firma, Maris and Mantle are chasing the Babe's single-season home run record. On the small screen, a hapless man named Wilbur holds secret discourse with a talking horse named Mr. Ed, and at the movies, the Absent-Minded Professor has just invented flubber. We are still light-years away from Eminem, and Nelly, and "It's gettin hot in here, so take off all your clothes." No, no, our transistor radio is playing Dion & the Belmonts, who are warning against the feminine wiles of a girl named Runaround Sue, and the Shirelles ask, demurely, that musical question on the mind of every teenage girl being driven in a Chevy Impala up to Lover's Lane: "Will you still love me tomorrow?"

Yet as we climb into our cuddly feet pajamas of mid-century nostalgia, let's not forget that this is also the year that the CIA superimposes a bull's-eye on the face of Fidel Castro, feeds fiction to the public, and sends bankrolled dissidents to the Bay of Pigs to accomplish what will be a dangerously miscalculated attempt at "regime change." Across the Atlantic, in Berlin, a twenty-five-mile barbed wire fence is being erected to separate East from West. In response, the president pre-empts *Mr. Ed* to warn Americans that the escalating crisis may result in a Soviet nuclear attack on our soil. His speech triggers a national preoccupation with homeland security, and the backyard bomb shelter, that quaint concrete cousin of the plastic and duct tape shroud, becomes the trend du jour. On the civil rights front, the Freedom Riders travel by bus from Washington to New Orleans to desegregate the South. En route they are met with bombs and beatings by men in hoods. Because racism is a legacy, not a genetic predisposition, one of these hooded bullies will, perhaps, sire a son who will sire a son who will scrawl anonymous hate graffiti on a college bulletin board in New London, Connecticut, nearly forty years hence. Racists, anti-Semites, gay-bashers, Arab-trashers: no matter what the era, no matter who the target, the hatemonger is cut from the same cloth of inferior weave.

But as for me, if it's 1961, then I am ten years old, a fifth grader living just up the road in Norwich, Connecticut. At school, I'm learning how to diagram sentences, master long division, and execute the duck-and-cover exercises which somehow will save me when the Soviets drop the bomb on the submarine base in Groton. I won't write my first fiction for another twenty years, but the seeds of my storyteller's life are planted this year by a scary nun named Sister Mercy.

You see, my mother, who is alive again and dark-haired, insists that I attend catechism class at St. Patrick's School each Wednesday afternoon from 3:30 to 4:30. Having already spent the day with three dozen parochial school students, Sister Mercy is not happy to see three dozen more rowdy public school students tramping in. We are equally unhappy to be there. There is acting out, screaming, rulers slapped against desktops, spitballs launched from the barrels of ballpoint pens. And as Sister patrols the aisles, one of us catechists, a wild girl named Pauline Migliaccio, goes so far as to affix a paper sign to the back of her veil. "Shake It, Don't Break It," the sign says, and so that you might appreciate the full-fledged audacity of

Pauline's act, may I remind you that we're still decades away from the invention of the Post-it note.

Unlike Pauline Migliaccio, I am far too timid to make trouble for Sister Mercy. My modus operandi for survival is to sit in back, say nothing, and try as best I can to blend in with the wainscoting. But on the afternoon my fate as a fiction writer is sealed, I get a strange and inexplicable urge. I want Sister to like me. Or, if she cannot like me, then at least to notice I exist. And so, at 4:30, when she intones those liberating words, "Class dismissed," my peers lurch toward the exit, and I hang back. I stand. With a wildly thumping heart, I approach Sister's big wooden desk.

She is correcting papers and scowling—doesn't notice at first that I stand facing her. And when she does look up, she says, "Yes, what is it?"

I don't really know what it is, but she has spent a good part of the last hour talking about the Vatican. "Sister," I say. "My grandfather moved to America from Italy in 1890." True. He did. Pure, unadulterated nonfiction. But I can see from Sister's clenched face that she is unimpressed.

My knees knock; my mind ricochets. Now, as it happens, earlier this same day, two of my public-school classmates brought into class a papier-mâché volcano. They poured baking soda into the core, added vinegar, and made lava bubble up, spring forth, and dribble down the sides. And this demonstration suddenly comes to mind.

"And, Sister . . . before Grandpa came over? When he was still living in Italy? This volcano erupted in his town. It was early in the morning, and he was the only one awake, and so he pounded on people's doors and everyone escaped and so he saved a whole bunch of people's lives."

Sister's facial muscles relax. She cocks her head. Her

gold-rim glasses glint a little from the light of the fluorescent lamp above. But I can see that my marriage of falsehood and fact has fallen just short of being enough. It's a moment of truth. A moment suspended in time. Sister looks at me and waits. I look back at her and wait. And then, finally, I add . . .

"And . . . the pope gave him a medal."

She nods, she smiles. She reaches into her bottom desk drawer, removes a holy picture, and presents it to me. The following Wednesday afternoon, Sister knows my name, I have preferred seating up front, and for the rest of this school year, whenever there is need for a note to travel from Sister Mercy's room to the office, you can probably guess who is chosen to deliver it.

And so, at the tender age of ten, I learn of the rich rewards that can be yours if you take the truth and lie like hell about it. Bend it to your liking. Now, I could have become a Connecticut politician, I suppose. But no, I became first a teacher, and later a fiction writer.

But what do fiction writers know, Mr. Journalist has e-mailed me to ask. Why should anyone listen to them? Because, says Grace Paley, "A writer must be truthful. A story is a big lie. And in the middle of this big lie, you're telling the truth." Because, says novelist Jessamyn West, "Fiction reveals the truth that reality obscures." "Why shouldn't truth be stranger than fiction?" Mark Twain observes. "Fiction, after all, has to make sense."

Fast-forward. It's 1984. Ronald Reagan, Boy George, break dancing, big hair. That new NBA rookie, Michael Jordan, seems so effortlessly airborne that it's as if he's affixed flubber to his sneaker bottoms. I'm thirty-three now. I've been both a father and a fiction writer for three years; one calling has somehow unleashed the other. You see, as I study my small son

Jared and try to imagine who he will grow up to become, I begin to get these characters' voices in my head. I write down what these figments say and start to worry about them and root for their safety as if they were real. The catch is: I can only find out what's happening to them when their voices spill from the pointy end of my Bic pen onto the loose-leaf pages in front of me. And as I work on these stories, I defy as best I can that other voice of self-inflicted doubt, which keeps whispering, Stop kidding yourself. You're never going to get anything published. Get real. Get up from that desk and mow the lawn.

But I've let the lawn grow and toiled away for three years and now, in 1984, the phone rings. It's Lary Bloom, the editor of the *Hartford Courant's Northeast* magazine. He wants to publish one of my short stories—the one about the fat woman, Dolores. When my conversation with the editor ends, I hang up the phone and dance my wife around the kitchen. I pick up three-year-old Jared and toss him so high into the air that his head hits the ceiling. But, hey, it's okay because it's one of those suspended ceilings with the lightweight panels, so Jared's head isn't hurt; it just disappears for a second. My short story is published on Easter Sunday. I drive at dawn to the convenience store and buy three *Hartford Courants.* For ten minutes I can't bear to look. Then I do look. I sit there by myself in the strip mall parking lot and cry like an idiot. I am on my way.

Zoom zoom. It's 1999. Kosovo, the Clinton scandal, the slaughter of students at Columbine High. My fiction has been twice touched by the magic wand of the Oprah Winfrey Book Club, and so my character Dolores has relocated from my hard drive to the best-seller list. The troubled identical twins I've worried into existence for my second novel have followed suit and so I am preparing to take off on a cross-country book tour. Meanwhile, Jared has metamorphosed from that airborne three-year-old into a six-foot-two high school senior, a near-man of seventeen. He helps me heft my luggage out to the driveway where a purring limousine waits. And as I'm driven away, I look through the tinted rear window at my child and, again, I am wet-eyed.

I see a young man coauthored out of love—a son who, having moved recently into his adult body, is receding from me, but who I once knew better than I know myself—better than he knew himself, certainly, because he has been, and in my mind remains, that arm-flailing infant on the changing table and the potbellied toddler in training pants. As he stands there in the present moment, he cannot possibly know that he is simultaneously, for me, the boy in the bowl cut clutching He-Man and Skeletor . . . the Webelos scout in the untucked uniform . . . the catcher of polliwogs in his squishy sneakers . . . the afternoon paperboy, the strap of his canvas bag crossing his chest like a bandolier . . . the zookeeper of a never-ending domestic menagerie: turtles, fish, fiddler crabs, two "female" gerbils—and their five or six hundred offspring. "Gee," one of his middle school teachers had told him. "You like people and animals so much, you ought to be a biology teacher."

But at seventeen, Jared doesn't know what he wants to be, or even where he wants to go to school next year—Bates, Bowdoin, Trinity, how's he supposed to know? Oh, and Connecticut College is on his list. He likes that cross-country coach down there, that Coach Butler. And that Coach Wuyke, too. He wouldn't mind running for those guys. But, hey, first things first. He can't even think of what to write for his stinking college admission essay.

On my book tour, in city after city, the crowds come out. Strangers who have read my novels ask me how I knew their lives, their flaws, their family secrets. And, of course, I've known none of these. I've only gone to work each day and told the lie that I am someone other than myself: a wounded girl trying to survive rape, an Italian immigrant with an ego larger than Sicily, the frightened identical twin of a schizophrenic brother. I have, each day in solitude, shucked my own life and put on different lives so that I might move beyond the limitations of my own experience and better empathize with, better know, the un-me, the other.

The novelist John Edgar Wideman has said, "I seek in fiction some hint that imagination can change the world, that the world is unfinished, a hint that we are not always doomed to make copies and copies and copies but possess the power to see differently and the guts and good fortune to render accessible to others some glimmer of what our own souls experience. Stories, after all, are a gift. Unless we're willing to imagine what it might feel like inside another skin, then we are imprisoned in our own."

By the time the limo delivers me back home again two weeks later, Jared has written his college essay. "Dad," he says, "can you check this for spelling?" And God knows, he needs it checked. Seventeen years old and he's still spelling the word "tomorrow" with two m's. But as I proofread, my attention shifts from mechanics to content. I'm surprised—I'm moved— to read that my son's essay too focuses on "the other": a girl on the front page of last year's newspaper—an innocent eleven-year-old Latina named Angelica who lived in our town and who loved to dance and who was stalked, raped, and murdered by a pedophile. Angelica and Jared were strangers to one another, born seven years apart. What they had in common was that each had walked the same steps of that paper route; each had played at that polliwog-filled pond where Angelica's body was later found. In his essay, Jared describes a solitary visit to the pond, where a granite boulder has become a makeshift memorial to Angelica. He writes:

The rock appeared to be alive with color, light, and movement. Pink rosary beads, purple flowers. Expired candles coat the rock with blue, green, and orange wax and, on the ground, a few flames still flicker with life. A plain white sheet of paper is Scotch-taped to the rock. In bold red letters its one word sums up all my feelings: WHY?

Mr. Journalist, fiction writers have no answers, only questions, the most succinct and significant of which is: WHY?

Why, God, if You exist and are merciful, must our loved ones be claimed by cancer, addiction, AIDS, mental illness, muscular dystrophy, murder? Why, America, if justice is blind, do we imprison the descendants of slaves in such disproportionate numbers? Why must our poorest children get the poorest education and our hungriest be denied a place at the banquet table? Why, suicide bomber? Why?

Tough questions, graduates. Unanswerable, many of them, no matter what your major—no matter what your grade point average. And yet we grope, we struggle to understand why. That struggle, I believe, is what makes us not just human but humane. And it can be a noble struggle when accompanied by a rejection of the unacceptable, unimaginative status quo and an honest effort to change things for the better. But how to improve an imperfect world, an imperfect nation, our imperfect selves? That question has occupied the minds of scholars, scientists, artists, and activists throughout time—and has sometimes . . . sometimes . . . been the pebble in the shoe that becomes the unbearable pain that motivates good minds and generous hearts to bring their gifts to the table, roll up their sleeves, and fix things. Graduates, be a part of that. Find work that adds to the world instead of depleting it. You owe that to yourselves, and to those descendants whose DNA you store inside you, and to the descendants of the un-you, the other.

Here we are back at the station—back in the uneasy present. What's that line from *The Matrix*? "Welcome to the desert of the real." As for the future, you'll have to get there yourselves. But before you depart, I offer you a modest travel gift: these few things a father and fiction writer knows.

Aubrey, Vlado, Maylynn, Britt: In life, as in writing, voice is crucial. Your voice has been honed by your family, your ethnic heritage, your neighborhood, and your education. It is the music of your meaning in the world. Imitate no one. Your uniqueness—your authenticity—is your strength.

Sarah, Oslec, Miranda, John: Make yours a life story which is character-driven, not plot-driven, character being defined as the way you behave when there is no one else in the room to judge you. Don't fear that silent room. Solitude will guide you if you remain strong of character.

Meghan, Justin, Alex, Joe: Learn to love the editing process. Listen to criticism, welcome it with gratitude and humility, but beware the false critic with a covert agenda. Make mistakes, lots of them, reworking draft after draft after draft of your continuing story. Your errors will be educational, and if your pencil outlives its eraser, then you'll know you're getting it right.

Clancy, Becca, Mridula, Jose: Regarding plot—the twists and turns and episodes of your life—outline as much or as little as you like, but expect surprise. In fact, invite surprise. Each time you begin some next chapter, your composition of yourself will be at risk. But that's okay—that's good—because you will not live fully if you never displace yourself. "Writing a novel is like driving a car at night," E. L. Doctorow once said.

"You may be able to see only as far as your headlights, but you can make the whole trip that way."

And finally, Jared, a personal word to you: You have been a most enjoyable child to raise. Levelheaded, playful, kind to others, you've made few missteps, and no unforgivable ones, with the exception of that time you rented that white tux, tails, and top hat for your senior prom. As you prepare now to board the bus—to take the Freedom Ride down to New Orleans to teach biology in one of the most forsaken school districts in the nation—please know that your family loves you and is proud of you and the work you've chosen. Keep in mind that the best teachers are the ones who love the student as much as the subject matter—the ones who stop speaking long enough to listen. Teaching will teach you, again and again, that you are the other and the other is you, despite the barriers we erect and the bombs we drop. Draw strength from the knowledge that education will break the backs of poverty, disenfranchisement, and violence; that war is never inevitable but only a terrible failure of the imagination; and that love is stronger than hatred. As it says so beautifully in Corinthians:

> As a child, I saw it face to face
> Now I only know it in part
> Fractions in me of faith, hope, and love
> And of these three, love's the greatest beauty.

So, Jared, *vaya con Dios.* Be well. Be safe. And know that, in the end, I wrote these words not for Mr. Journalist but for you, and your classmates, and Angelica, together.

Best-selling author Wally Lamb's novels She's Come Undone *and* I Know This Much Is True *were selected for Oprah's Book Club, and he is the recipient of an NEA grant for fiction.*

DENNIS LEHANE

Wow, it's a big room.

When I was a little kid, my parents took me next door to the new, at the time, UMass Boston campus the weekend it opened. Where we're standing right now was, by the way, a strip mall back then.

And my mother told me later that it meant so much in their lives to see this place open, because now it meant she could afford to send her kids to college. Otherwise . . .

I just want to make sure everyone understands, before I get started. I dropped out of this school. I mean, you all get that, right?

My buddy Chris Mullen—who applied to UMass with me and attended UMass with me and dropped out of UMass with me—when he heard about this, you know, he said, "They give doctorates for playing Space Invaders and Missile Command these days?" He also said, "If they start giving them out for drinking beer, we'll rule the world."

I want to thank UMass in general. I want to thank Chancellor Jo Ann Gora and President Wilson, Associate Chancellor Kenneth Lemanski, in particular for bestowing this honor upon me. I've decided not to let it go to my head except for this weekend. Just one weekend, I'm going to ask everyone to address me as "Doctah."

Come Monday, though, I'll be back to being my normal, ego-less self. Actually, it could be hard, though. This has impressed my mother more than the whole Clint Eastwood movie/Academy Awards thing ever did, believe me. And like any good son, it's important to me to make my mom happy, my dad, too.

I graduated from high school twenty years ago with a less than spectacular GPA, so I'm not really sure why I'm here. I had no clearly defined career path, no sense of what I wanted to be or could be, and then I dropped out of the first two colleges that were kind enough to accept me. I look back on my late teens and my early twenties, and the phrase that occurs to me again and again is, "My poor parents."

So to stand before you all today and tell you to follow the strict career path of college to corporation to junior partner to corporate board would be, I feel, disingenuous. And if you don't know what "disingenuous" means, then the faculty here is really starting to slip.

I've been to a few commencements myself, sat where you're sitting, so let me dispense with the traditional bromides right off the bat: dare to dream, follow your heart, be true to your school, don't forget the values your family and your elders gave you, blah blah blah. I can't stand up here and do that.

You're about to go out into the world, and the world as we've left it for you is in pretty bad shape. Neoconservatives will have you believe that the solution is to get back to a rosy-hued 1950s-era America that never existed. Ultraliberals will have you believe the solution is to build a utopia of politically correct speech and politically correct values where nobody offends anyone and nobody does anything bad or messy. And as far as I can tell, everyone will die of total and utter boredom.

I see the world through your eyes and I think you must be

bewildered, because I'm bewildered. I ask myself, "Where do we turn for honor anymore?" Just honor. Forget justice, forget truth; we'll just take honor—people and organizations acting honorably. The last time I checked, no one expected honor of our government when given the chance to act honorably. During the recent sex-abuse scandal, the Church turned into a corporate board. And the corporate boards of the world are best exemplified by Halliburton, Enron, Tyco, and all the other robber barons who have wrecked our economy and dummied up behind the Fifth Amendment.

We have set a very bad example for you folks, very bad. We were supposed to make the world a better place, and instead, it seems more unstable than it has ever been.

The good news, though: It's always been this way. The world—since the dawn of time, since the first caveman sold his neighbor a faulty club and used the extra shekels to put a wide-screen plasma on the wall of his cave—the world has pretty much worked on the same overriding principle: "If it's not about the money, it's about the money."

Is this the world you want for yourself? I hope to God not. I hope you realize what the people doing their best to wreck this world have not, that it is not about the money and it's not about protecting the image of an institution or a government if the image is propagated on lies.

Honor is not Mother Teresa in Calcutta. That's beyond honor; that's sainthood. You don't have to shoot that high. Honor is not an impossible ideal, something beyond your grasp. Honor is day to day. It's minute by minute. If you have it, you live without question. Honor is not doing what is easy if it hurts a single soul. Honor has no room in its house for cynicism—skepticism, yes, always—but cynicism, no. It has no room in its house for greed, for the mindless pursuit of money or hollow success. Honor is the affirmative answer to one simple question you ask of yourself every day: "Did I behave with dignity and respect toward all living things?" That's the measure of honor and the measure of humanity.

If you're cynical, you'll say, "I wasn't honorable today because the world was just dishonorable toward me and I just had to fight back." Sorry, wrong answer. The measure of a human being lies in not what the world does to him or her, but rather, how he or she comports [himself or] herself within that world. When someone says, oh so cynically, oh so jaded, "The world is thus," you must reply, "No. Thus have we made the world."

It's been remarked upon by enough friends and acquaintances that I am a pretty self-sufficient guy, as a person who came from so-called humble origins to rise to a point where I occasionally have hung out with movie stars and my books were read by presidents—well, the presidents who actually, you know, read books. And it's true I can get really, really good seats for Patriots games. I guess I would be a poster child for those who make very good money trafficking in the myth of the self-made man, the pull-yourselves-up-by-your-bootstraps folks who shoveled code words like "American individualism" down our throats just when they're closing the door on our faces and leaving us to sleep at night out in the cold. You know, those guys.

I am not a self-made man. This self was made with the help of others. It is no mistake that of the three men in *Mystic River,* the one who turns out okay is Sean Devine, the one with solid loving parents. And it's true that Sean Devine was the most autobiographical character I have ever written, which quite frankly is why he was the most difficult, boring character I've ever tried to write, because I'm a pretty boring guy. I'm stable and boring.

Sean's parents, then, were a testament to my own parents. I wanted to pay tribute to good people who kept their heads down and worked two and sometimes three jobs to raise their kids and never complained, people who raised their children to do the same, to believe in self-reliance and particularly a lack of whining, but—and this is so important—raised us to be very aware how much of self-reliance comes down to luck. The luck not to need a helping hand. The luck not to be completely alone in this world. The luck to have been born the right color at the right time in the right country.

In essence, my parents taught me empathy, not sympathy. Sympathy is easy. It's always given from a position of power. You sympathize for someone, the starving child on the late-night infomercial, the person who lost their trailer in a tornado, whoever the hell's on *American Idol* this week. But when you have empathy, you empathize with the person. You put yourself on equal footing. Sympathy is easy; empathy is hard.

I remember driving with my father once, and someone cut us off and I got all hot and asked why he wasn't beeping his horn or flipping the guy off. And my father said, "You don't know what type of day he's had." And I looked into the other car and I suddenly didn't see the jerk who'd cut us off in traffic. I saw a weary-looking guy with a weary-looking wife and two cranky kids in a battered old car, and I felt that there but for the grace of God go I. That's empathy.

Since 9/11, something happened to empathy in this country. I don't know what exactly, but it ain't good. I know that I wrote a novel in which all the characters have perfectly good and understandable reasons to be angry and they only commit acts of violence and vengeance once they're sure they're right. And yet, they're all wrong. I think human beings are at their most dangerous when they lose their empathy, when they objectify other human beings, when they are so sure they are right they feel justified in a take-no-prisoners attitude. And I don't know when mercy and decency became signs of weakness in this country.

This—what you see around you right now, what you're graduating from—this is welfare. Public education is a form of public welfare, a form of public assistance. The great and wise once decided that it was the duty of any great city or state to provide education for their citizenry—and not just so-so education, but a solid, even exemplary education like you get here, that some people still manage to drop out of, imagine that. So when the state or the city gives a helping hand to their populace, that is, yes, public welfare. So next time you think about demanding that someone pull himself up by his bootstraps, ask yourself if you did, or did you have some help? From your parents, from the state, from this school.

There is an angry, loud, and unfortunately popular, contingent in this country that will have you believe empathy and mercy are for the weak. They will have you believe that, even though their loudest mouths all come from wealth and the only bootstraps they ever pulled were made of imported Italian leather. They will have you believe that the future of this country lies in the lack of a helping hand and the striking motion of an angry one. This contingent has made themselves popular by feeding off our inherent need for anger. They offer no solutions with the exception of placing more wealth in the hands of those who don't need it, or put another way, I need another tax break like Johnny Damon needs more hair.

Meanwhile, they assail everything that was good and American and pure in this country. The right to free speech, the right to love whoever you choose, the privilege of helping others less fortunate, of educating our children, of assuring a good life for our elderly, of caring for our sick. They want to privatize education and privatize Medicare and privatize you right out of every good thing that makes this country great. I know another word for privatize, but I can't use it because my mom's here and I never swear in front of my mother.

Make no mistake about it. These are the same people whose ancestors and ideological compatriots from eighty years ago were against Social Security, affordable health care, workers' comp, disability insurance, pensions, the eight-hour day, the forty-hour week, the weekend, women's right to vote, blacks' right to vote, integration, special benefits for veterans—all of this, while they wrap themselves in the flag and tell us what America is.

So you remember that the next time someone pulls out the libel by label card and trots out tired, meaningless clichés about liberalism and their doctrine: Ask them what they stand for. Not what they stand against. What they stand for. And if all they can come up with is some lame BS about a family-values world, where the family is white and wealthy and the values are something you decree while driving your Humvee to the golf course, then ask them to please keep driving that Humvee over the Mexican border and out of our country, because that's not an America I would send my sons to die for.

Look around at yourselves, right now, all of you. This is America, you. You're America. You're truly its best and its brightest, because you had to work for your education, because you know that just getting this education means someone in the state empathized with you without ever meeting you. And you have to give that empathy back. You're America, and you're white and you're black and you're toffee-colored, and you're Asian and Indo-Asian, Slavic-American, with a Frenchman somewhere back in the woodpile.

You are your parents and their parents, and they worked hard so their offspring could work hard so that you could be born here and go to this school, and graduate with all the other offspring who can trace their ancestry back to northern Europe or the Russian steppes, or Honduras or Manchuria or Yemen, or the Dutch Antilles and every single place in between.

Anytime you engage in looking down on anyone, categorizing anyone for any reasons to do with race, class, sexual preference, anytime you presuppose that you know best for a population that you share little in common with, then you have disengaged from empathy. And lack of empathy, ladies and gentlemen, is un-American.

So take your hopes and your dreams out into the world. Take your intellect, which has been finely honed here, I hope, but don't forget your hearts. Don't forget your compassion, don't forget your honor, and don't forget your empathy.

Thank you very much.

Best-selling author Dennis Lehane is known for his gritty crime novels, set mainly in Boston. Mystic River *was made into a successful film.*

FRANK MCCOURT

Connecticut College, 1999

The question is, should I talk about you or should I talk about me? If I talk about you, I might begin to sound like a commencement speaker. I might start exhorting you to "go forth." Commencement speakers like to say "go forth." You're going anyway. You are not going to sit in this sun for the rest of your life! And the main thing on your minds is to get your diploma and get out of the sun and go to lunch with your loved ones. You'll have a big lunch, and you will think of this day even ten or twenty years from now as one of the turning points of your life. If I talk about you, I might start giving you some advice, and I am very poor at giving advice. As Oscar Wilde said, "The best thing to do with advice is to give it to someone else; you can't use it yourself." So I can't give you any advice, because after thirty years of teaching high school English in New York City, I found that when I gave kids advice they may have taken it in, but they didn't always follow it. So I just learned to present something to them. And what I presented was what I knew, or what I thought I knew.

I could talk about myself, and then if I talk about myself, I am talking about you, because although I never had the experience that you are having, I did go to college, but I never went to high school. I skipped that. You could have done that too if you were wise. I did it, and if I can do it anyone can do it. And that's why I feel a little guilty standing here this morning. I feel nervous because I am in the presence of such accomplished people, such educated people. This class sitting before me, your minds are brimming with the knowledge you have gained in the last four years. You have gained facts and skills, and I hope that there is a strong underpinning of wisdom, and nudging the wisdom aside is a sense of adventure, which I hope you will have. Because it doesn't end here. You might go for a master's or you might go for a PhD, but even then it doesn't end.

I didn't know when I landed in New York at the age of nineteen what was going to happen to me. I had no idea whatsoever. There was no one standing there inviting me to come to Connecticut College. As a matter of fact, I think if I had applied here they would have laughed and turned me away because I didn't have any credentials. I didn't know what I was going to do. I floundered awhile, like many immigrants. I am sure some of you had people in your family like that—your parents, your grandparents, people who came to this country who floundered awhile and then found a place in American society.

I had a series of menial jobs, and then I was liberated from those menial jobs by China. China attacked Korea, and America got nervous and turned to me and drafted me. But I wasn't sent to Korea, because they didn't want the war to end too soon. They sent me to Germany—that was really the beginning of my teaching career. They had me training attack dogs, German shepherds. I had to train them to be mean. We used Russian uniforms and hit the dogs on the noses with the Russian uniforms so that the dogs would hate Russians. So my first introduction to teaching was the teaching of hatred to German shepherds.

When I was discharged from the army, I think the best thing

that ever happened to me was the gift of the GI Bill. I don't know if you are old enough to know anything about the GI Bill, but at the end of the Second World War and the end of the Korean War, the government provided educational benefits for veterans. I didn't have a high school diploma, I had never been in a high school, so how could I go to college? I'll tell you how. I used to live in Greenwich Village, not far from my mama. I would go to a tavern called the White Horse, where Dylan Thomas drank himself to death. I wasn't proposing to do that myself. I went into this bar one day when I was working on the docks, and I was a bit weary of the laboring life. I was having a beer and a knockwurst. And I did something that no young Irishman should ever do. I began to ask myself, what is the meaning of it all? And that is a dangerous thing to do when you are having a beer and a knockwurst. The most dangerous part of it, and the saddest part of it, was I got slightly depressed and got off my bar stool. I walked away from my half-empty beer and my half-eaten knockwurst and walked to Washington Square, and there was New York University. Maybe it was because of the half beer I had, but I said to myself, I think I will go there. And I went to the admission office to get me a form. I filled out the form, and they said, "What about the high school? You didn't fill out the high school part." I said, "I never went to high school, but I think I am very intelligent." That was a very arrogant thing to say, but I was desperate to get into NYU, or to any college. There was a dean passing by, and she said, "Well, what is going on here?" And they said, "Well, he claims he's very intelligent." I had told them that I had read a lot of books, and they wanted to know what books. I trotted out an impressive list of books, whether I had read them or not. I emphasized Voltaire very heavily. He's a big one. He said, "Cultivate your garden." That is one of my favorite sayings. So they let me in on probation for a year. I didn't sail in the way you sailed into Connecticut College. Not that I sailed out the way you are doing. I had to work during my years as a student. And along the way I decided to become a teacher, because there wasn't anything else that appealed to me. I think the life of a writer appealed to me, but I didn't have the courage nor did I have the skill at the time. So I thought combining my love of books with my love of kids would become the perfect life for me, so I'll become a teacher.

In the thirty years that I was teaching in various high schools in New York, I started at one of the hardest in the city, a technical high school for the kids who were not interested in listening to me babble on about *Silas Marner,* which they call the dirty old man book. They would not listen. There were kids in auto mechanics and machine shop and all these different trades, and I had to hold their attention. That's the kind of skill you have to develop as a teacher and as an actor—finding a way to hold the attention of the audience the way I have you now—in the palm of my hands—by describing this journey. Nobody told me how to teach. Nobody can tell you how to teach. Actually nobody can tell you anything. You have to find it out for yourself. I know you have a college degree, or you will in a few minutes, as soon as I stop talking. In the long run, I have discovered, you have to struggle along as a teacher, or an actor, a writer, or anything else.

But I look back at the thirty years of teaching and know that was the best thing I ever did in my life, I think. I had to deal with the young people of all economic levels, of all shades of intelligence. I had to struggle. I had to learn about the American teenager. I had to learn about literature. In the long run what I was learning was something about myself, and above all, about the human heart. My experience as a teacher was the experience as a student. I became a teacher and I began my education in the classroom. I began to know something about myself. That's the main thing you have to know—thyself. "Presume not God to scan; the proper study of mankind is man." This is what I discovered, and I think the kids helped me. As soon as I opened my mouth they would ask, "You Scotch or something?" and I had to admit that I was Irish. They regarded me as kind of an exotic, and they wanted to know about my life. I told them. They wanted to know about my education, religion, sports, and girls and everything else. You are told by other teachers, "Don't tell the students anything about your private life." But they wanted to know. And because I was telling them, stories were forming in my head. Students would say to me, "Hey, Mr. McCourt, you should write a book." And I did. I do what I'm told. That was the main thing about teaching. I don't know how many of you are intending on becoming teachers. I used to ask the senior high school class every year, "How many of you intend to become teachers?" In eighteen years, only two hands were raised. The possessors of the two hands were not a very likeable pair. One of them, I think, was a potential serial killer, and I don't know what the other one was, but I wouldn't have them in the classroom. Unfortunately, the teaching profession was not glamorous enough nor was it well paid enough. But for me, it was glamorous, for me it was well paid. I know you know that teachers' salaries are very low compared with starlets on soap operas and jobs like that. I know you know that and maybe not too many of you are drawn to teaching, but I have to thank all those years in the classroom, I have to thank approximately eleven thousand students that I had and thirty-three thousand lessons that I taught. I learned; I learned over the years. But although I learned, I wondered if I knew anything in the long run. I've written a best-seller and I have finished another book. Now I have to write another one. I don't know what—you get this itch and you don't know what to do with yourself so you have to write a best-seller. Which is to be made into a major motion picture, with all—and I might even be surrounded by all—I might even meet Sharon Stone. How higher can you aspire to than that?

I stand on the stage with the graduates of Connecticut College and the distinguished members of the faculty and the recipients of honorary degrees, and all I can tell you is that I am living the American dream, and you have contributed to it. Thank you very much.

Frank McCourt was a high school teacher before he wrote his memoir Angela's Ashes *and won the Pulitzer Prize for biography; the book was an international best-seller.*

TONI MORRISON

I have to confess to all of you, Madame President, Board of Trustees, members of the faculty, relatives, friends, students, I have had some conflicted feelings about accepting this invitation to deliver the commencement address to Wellesley's Class of 2004. My initial response, of course, was glee, a very strong sense of pleasure at, you know, participating personally and formally in the rites of an institution with this reputation, one hundred twenty-five years of history in women's education, an enviable rostrum of graduates, its commitment sustained over the years in making a difference in the world and its successful resistance to challenges that women's colleges have faced from the beginning and throughout the years, an extraordinary record, and I was delighted to be asked to participate and return to this campus.

But my second response was not so happy. I was very anxious about having to figure out something to say to this particular class at this particular time, because I was really troubled by what could be honestly said in 2004 to over five hundred elegantly educated women, or to relatives and friends who are relieved at this moment, but hopeful as well as apprehensive. And to a college faculty and administration dedicated to leadership and knowledgeable about what that entails. Well, of course, I could be sure of the relatives and the friends, just tell them that youth is always insulting because it manages generation after generation not only to survive and replace us, but to triumph over us completely.

And I would remind the faculty and the administration of what each knows: that the work they do takes second place to nothing, nothing at all, and that theirs is a first-order profession. Now, of course, to the graduates I could make reference to things appropriate to your situations—the future, the past, the present, but most of all happiness. Regarding the future, I would have to rest my case on some bromide, like the future is yours for the taking. Or—that it's whatever you make of it. But the fact is, it is not yours for the taking. And it is not whatever you make of it. The future is also what other people make of it. How other people will participate in it and impinge on your experience of it.

But I'm not going to talk anymore about the future, because I'm hesitant to describe or predict, because I'm not even certain that it exists. That is to say, I'm not certain that somehow, perhaps, a burgeoning ménage à trois of political interests, corporate interests, and military interests will not prevail and literally annihilate an inhabitable, humane future. Because I don't think we can any longer rely on separation of powers, free speech, religious tolerance, or unchallengeable civil liberties as a matter of course. That is, not while finite humans in the flux of time make decisions of infinite damage. Not while finite humans make infinite claims of virtue and unassailable power that are beyond their competence, if not their reach. So—no happy talk about the future.

Maybe the past offers a better venue. You already share an old tradition of an uncompromisingly intellectual women's college, and that past and that tradition is important to both understand and preserve. It's worthy of reverence and transmission. You've already learned some strategies for appraising the historical and economical and cultural past that you have inherited. But this is not a speech focusing on the splendor of the national past that you are also inheriting.

You will detect a faint note of apology in the descriptions of this bequest. A kind of sorrow that accompanies it, because it's not good enough for you. Because the past is already in debt to the mismanaged present. And besides, contrary to what you may have heard or learned, the past is not done and it is not over, it's still in process, which is another way of saying that when it's critiqued, analyzed, it yields new information about itself. The past is already changing as it is being reexamined, as it is being listened to for deeper resonances. Actually, it can be more liberating than any imagined future if you are willing to identify its evasions, its distortions, its lies, and are willing to unleash its secrets.

But again, it seemed inappropriate, very inappropriate for me to delve into a past for people who are in the process of making one, forging their own, so I considered focusing on your responsibility as graduates—as graduates of this institution and citizens of the world, and to tell you once again, repeat to you the admonition, a sort of a wish, that you go out and save the world. That is, to suggest to you that with energy and right thinking you can certainly improve, certainly you might even rescue it. Now that's a heavy burden to be placed on one generation by a member of another generation, because it's a responsibility we ought to share, not save the world, but simply to love it, meaning don't hurt it, it's already beaten and scoured and gasping for breath. Don't hurt it or enable others who do and will. Know and identify the predators waving flags made of dollar bills. They will say anything, promise anything, do everything to turn the planet into a casino where only the house cards can win—little people with finite lives love to play games with the infinite. But I thought better of that, selecting your responsibilities for you. If I did that, I would assume your education had been in vain and that you were incapable of deciding for yourself what your responsibilities should be.

So I'm left with the last thing that I sort of ignored as a topic. Happiness. I'm sure you have been told that this is the best time of your life. It may be. But if it's true that this is the best time of your life, if you have already lived or are now living at this age the best years, or if the next few turn out to be the best, then you have my condolences. Because you'll want to remain here, stuck in these so-called best years, never maturing, wanting only to look, to feel, and be the adolescent that whole industries are devoted to forcing you to remain.

One more flawless article of clothing, one more elaborate toy, the truly perfect diet, the harmless but necessary drug, the almost final elective surgery, the ultimate cosmetic—all designed to maintain hunger for stasis. While children are being eroticized into adults, adults are being exoticized into eternal juvenilia. I know that happiness has been the real, if covert, target of your labors here. Your choices of companions or the profession that you will enter, you deserve it and I want you to gain it, everybody should. But if that's all you have on your mind, then you do have my sympathy, and if these are indeed the best years of your life, you do have my condolences because there is nothing, believe me, more satisfying, more gratifying than true adulthood. The adulthood that is the span of life before you. The process of becoming one is not inevitable. Its achievement is a difficult beauty, an intensely hard-won glory, which commercial forces and cultural vapidity should not be permitted to deprive you of.

Now, if I can't talk inspiringly and hopefully about the future or the past or the present and your responsibility to the present or happiness, you might be wondering why I showed up. If things are that dour, that tentative, you might ask yourself, what's this got to do with me? What about my life? I didn't ask to be born, as they say. I beg to differ with you. Yes, you did! In fact, you insisted upon it. It's too easy, you know, too ordinary, too common to not be born. So your presence here on Earth is a very large part your doing.

So it is to the self, that self that insisted on life, that I want to speak now—candidly—and tell you. The truth is that I have not really been clearheaded about the world I have described to you, the one you are inheriting. All my ruminations about the future, the past, responsibility, happiness are really about my generation, not yours. My generation's profligacy, my generation's heedlessness and denial, its frail ego that required endless draughts of power juice and repeated images of weakness in others in order to prop up our own illusion of strength. More and more self-congratulation while we sell you more and more games and images of death as entertainment. In short, the palm I was reading wasn't yours, it was the splayed hand of my own generation, and I know no generation has a complete grip on the imagination and work of the next one, not mine and not your parents', not if you refuse to let it be so—you don't have to accept those media labels. You need not settle for any defining category. You don't have to be merely a taxpayer or a red state or a blue state or a consumer or a minority or a majority.

Of course you're general, but you're also specific. A citizen and a person, and the person you are is like nobody else on the planet. Nobody has the exact memory that you have. What is now known is not all of what you are capable of knowing. You are your own stories and therefore free to imagine and experience what it means to be human without wealth. What it feels like to be human without domination over others, without reckless arrogance, without fear of others unlike you, without rotating, rehearsing, and reinventing the hatreds you learned in the sandbox. And although you don't have complete control over the narrative (no author does, I can tell you), you could nevertheless create it.

Although you will never fully know or successfully manipulate the characters who surface or disrupt your plot, you can respect the ones who do by paying them close attention and doing them justice. The theme you choose may change or simply elude you, but being your own story means you can always choose the tone. It also means that you can invent the language to say who you are and how you mean. But then, I am a teller of stories and therefore an optimist, a believer in the ethical bend of the human heart, a believer in the mind's disgust with fraud and its appetite for truth, a believer in the ferocity of beauty, so from my point of view, which is that of a storyteller, I see your life as already artful, waiting, just waiting and ready for you to make it art.

Thank you.

Toni Morrison debuted as a novelist in 1970. She was the first black woman to win the Nobel Prize for Literature and is a recipient of the Pulitzer Prize for Beloved.

SALMAN RUSHDIE

Bard College, 1996

A Commencement Address

Members of the Class of 1996, I see in the newspaper that Southampton University on Long Island got Kermit the Frog to give the commencement address this year. You, unfortunately, have to make do with me. The only Muppet connection I can boast is that my former editor at Alfred Knopf was also the editor of that important self-help text, *Miss Piggy's Guide to Life.* I once asked him how it had been to work with such a major star and he replied, reverentially, "Salman: The pig was divine."

In England, where I went to college, we don't do things quite this way on graduation day, so I've been doing a little research into commencement and its traditions. The first American friend I asked told me that in her graduation year— not at this college, I hasten to add—she and her fellow students were so incensed at the choice of commencement speaker, whom I suppose I should not name—oh, all right then, it was Jeane Kirkpatrick—that they boycotted the ceremony and staged a sit-in in one of the college buildings instead. It is a considerable relief, therefore, to note that you are all here.

As for myself, I graduated from Cambridge University in 1968—the great year of student protest—and I have to tell you that I almost didn't make it. This story has nothing to do with politics or demonstrations; it is, rather, the improbable and cautionary tale of a thick brown gravy-and-onion sauce. It begins a few nights before my graduation day, when some anonymous wit chose to redecorate my room, in my absence, by hurling a bucketful of the aforesaid gravy-and-onions all over the walls and furniture, to say nothing of my record player and my clothes. With that ancient tradition of fairness and justice upon which the colleges of Cambridge pride themselves, my college instantly held me solely responsible for the mess, ignored all my representations to the contrary, and informed me that unless I paid for the damage before the ceremony, I would not be permitted to graduate. It was the first, but, alas, not the last occasion on which I would find myself wrongly accused of muckspreading. I paid up, I have to report, and was therefore declared eligible to receive my degree; in a defiant spirit, possibly influenced by my recent gravy experience, I went to the ceremony wearing brown shoes, and was promptly plucked out of the parade of my gowned and properly black-shod contemporaries and ordered back to my quarters to change.

I am not sure why people in brown shoes were deemed to be dressed improperly, but once again I was facing a judgment against which there could be no appeal. Once again, I gave in, sprinted off to change my shoes, got back to the parade in the nick of time; and at length, after these vicissitudes, when my turn came, I was required to hold a university officer by his little finger, and to follow him slowly up to where the vice-chancellor sat upon a mighty throne. As instructed, I knelt at his feet, held up my hands, palms together, in a gesture of supplication, and begged in Latin for the degree, for which, I could not help thinking, I had worked extremely hard for three years, supported by my family at considerable expense. I recall being advised to hold my hands way up above my head, in case the elderly vice-chancellor, leaning forward to clutch at them, should topple off his great chair and land on top of me. I did as I was advised; the elderly gentleman did not topple; and, also in Latin, he finally admitted me to the degree of Bachelor of Arts. Looking back at that day, I am a little appalled by my passivity, hard though it is to see what else I could have done. I could have not paid up, not changed my shoes, not knelt to supplicate for my BA. I preferred to surrender and get the degree.

I have grown more stubborn since.

I have come to the conclusion, which I now offer you, that I was wrong to compromise; wrong to make an accommodation with injustice, no matter how persuasive the reasons. Injustice, today, still conjures up in my mind the memory of gravy. Injustice, for me, is a brown, lumpy, congealing fluid, and it smells pungently, tearfully, of onions. Unfairness is the feeling of running back to your room, flat out, at the last minute, to change your outlawed brown shoes. It is the business of being forced to beg, on your knees, in a dead language, for what is rightfully yours. This, then, is what I learned on my own graduation day; this is the message I have derived from the parables of the Unknown Gravy-bomber, the Vetoed Footwear, and the Unsteady Vice-Chancellor upon his Throne, and which I pass on to you today: First, if, as you go through life, people should some day accuse you of what one might call aggravated gravy abuse—and they will, they will—and if in fact you are innocent of abusing gravy, do not take the rap. Second: Those who would reject you because you are wearing the wrong shoes are not worth being accepted by. And third: Kneel before no man. Stand up for your rights.

I like to think that Cambridge University, where I was so happy for three marvelous years, and from which I gained so much—I hope your years at Bard have been as happy, and that you feel you have gained as much—that Cambridge University, with its finely developed British sense of irony, intended me to learn precisely these valuable lessons from the events of that strange graduation day.

Members of the Class of 1996, we are here to celebrate with you one of the great days of your lives. We participate today in the rite of passage by which you are released from this life of preparation into that life for which you are now as prepared as anyone ever is. As you stand at the gate of the future, I should like to share with you a piece of information about the extraordinary institution you are leaving, which will explain the reason why it is such a particular pleasure for me to be with you today. In 1989, within weeks of the threat made against me by the mullahs of Iran, I was approached by the president of Bard, through my literary agent, and asked if I would consider accepting a place on the faculty of this college. More than a place; I was assured that I could find, here in Annandale, among the Bard community, many friends, and a safe haven in which I could live and work. Alas, I was not able, in those difficult days, to take up this courageous offer, but I have never forgotten that at a moment when red-alert signals were flashing all over the world, and all sorts of people and institutions were running scared, Bard College did the opposite—that it moved toward me, in intellectual solidarity and human concern, and made, not lofty speeches, but a concrete offer of help. I hope you will all feel proud that Bard, quietly, without fanfares, made such a principled gesture at such a time.

I am certainly extremely proud to be a recipient of Bard's

honorary degree, and to have been accorded the exceptional privilege of addressing you today. Hubris, according to the Greeks, was the sin of defying the gods, and could, if you were really unlucky, unleash against you the terrifying, avenging figure of the goddess Nemesis, who carried in one hand an apple bough and, in the other, the Wheel of Fortune, which would one day circle round to the inevitable moment of vengeance. As I have been, in my time, accused not only of gravy abuse and wearing brown shoes but of hubris, too, and since I have come to believe that such defiance is an inevitable and essential aspect of what we call freedom, I thought I might commend it to you. For in the years to come you will find yourselves up against gods of all sorts, big and little gods, corporate and incorporeal gods, all of them demanding to be worshipped and obeyed—the myriad deities of money and power, of convention and custom, that will seek to limit and control your thoughts and lives.

Defy them; that's my advice to you. Thumb your noses; cock your snooks. For, as the myths tell us, it is by defying the gods that human beings have best expressed their humanity. The Greeks tell many stories of quarrels between us and the gods. Arachne, the great artist of the loom, sets her skills of weaving and embroidery against those of the goddess of wisdom herself, Minerva or Pallas Athene; and impudently chooses to weave versions of only those scenes which reveal the mistakes and weaknesses of the gods—the rape of Europa, Leda and the Swan. For this—for the irreverence, not for her lesser skill; for what we would now call art, and chutzpah—the goddess changes her mortal rival into a spider. Queen Niobe of Thebes tells her people not to worship Latona, the mother of Diana and Apollo, saying, "What folly is this!—To prefer beings whom you never saw to those who stand before your eyes!" For this sentiment, which today we would call humanism, the gods murder her children and husband, and she metamorphoses into a rock, petrified with grief, from which there trickles an unending river of tears. Prometheus the Titan steals fire from the gods and gives it to mankind. For this—for what we would now call the desire for progress, for improved scientific and technological capabilities—he is bound to a rock while a great bird gnaws eternally at his liver, which regenerates as it is consumed.

The interesting point is that the gods do not come out of these stories at all well. If Arachne is overly proud when she seeks to compete with a goddess, it is only an artist's pride, joined to the gutsiness of youth; whereas Minerva, who could afford to be gracious, is merely vindictive. The story increases Arachne's shadow, as they say, and diminishes Minerva's. It is Arachne who gains, from the tale, a measure of immortality. And the cruelty of the gods to the family of Niobe proves her point. Who could prefer the rule of such cruel gods to self-rule, the rule of men and women by men and women, however flawed that may be? Once again, the gods are weakened by their show of strength, while the human beings grow stronger, even though—even as—they are destroyed. And tormented Prometheus, of course, Prometheus with his gift of fire, is the greatest hero of all.

It is men and women who have made the world, and they have made it in spite of their gods. The message of the myths is not the one the gods would have us learn—that we should behave ourselves and know our place—but its exact opposite. It is that we must be guided by our natures. Our worst natures can, it's true, be arrogant, venal, corrupt, or selfish; but in our best selves, we—that is, you—can and will be joyous, adventurous, cheeky, creative, inquisitive, demanding, competitive, loving, and defiant.

Do not bow your heads. Do not know your place. Defy the gods. You will be astonished how many of them turn out to have feet of clay. Be guided, if possible, by your better natures. Great good luck and many congratulations to you all.

Salman Rushdie has written novels, essays, short stories, and film criticism. His novel Midnight's Children *was selected in 1993 for the prestigious "Booker of Bookers" Prize, as the best in its twenty-five-year history.*